itr

A FRAGRANT ODYSSEY

VIPUL SURI

This is a work of nonfiction. The events and the incidents mentioned in the book are true and real. However, some names and characteristics have been changed, some events have been compressed, and some dialogues have been recreated.

First Edition: November 2023
Printed in India

Printed at PrintPlus Pvt. Ltd., Mumbai
Typeset in Adobe Garamond Pro

ISBN: 978-81-19445-94-3

Cover Design: Komal Lalwani

STORYMIRROR
Stories that reflect you

Publisher: StoryMirror Infotech Pvt. Ltd.
7th Floor, El Tara Building, Behind Delphi Building,
Hiranandani Gardens, Powai, Mumbai,
Maharashtra - 400076, India.

Web: storymirror.com
Facebook: @storymirror
Instagram: @storymirror
Twitter: @story_mirror
Contact Us: marketing@storymirror.com

About the Author

Dr. Kiranpreet Kaur is a trained Counselling Psychologist and founder of 'Celestial Wellness'; an organization working towards the holistic development and emotional wellbeing of students, teachers, parents and corporates. She has been working extensively from last 2 decades in the field of trainings, counselling and mental health. She encompasses the equilateral triangle consisting of parents, teachers and children well enough through workshops, seminars, & individual one to one sessions. Kiranpreet Kaur is well known as a Personal Impact Coach for bringing positive changes in her client's life by providing practical solutions.

Dr. Kiranpreet Kaur has been awarded with many prestigious awards like **Radha Krishnan Memorial Award** (A National Level Award) for her work in the field of teacher trainings and **Indian Healthcare Award** as the Most Promising Psychologist in Delhi for her contribution in the field of Mental Health & Wellbeing. She has done her training and Internship from Alpharetta International

Academy, Georgia, USA. She has worked as an editor with Amity University Press and works with multiple NGO's supporting various social causes. She has presented her research papers in many national and international conferences and appeared on many talk shows on Disha TV and Prime News Channel. Her sole mission is to spread awareness about the importance of mental health and emotional wellbeing to young generation and how to reach their full potential by tapping into their inner capabilities.

On personal front, she keeps on exploring her other innate qualities by doing and trying something out of the box every time she gets an opportunity. Participating and then becoming a Top Finalist in **Mrs. India Worldwide 2018**, conducted in Greece was one of such moves. In 2023, she was a participant in a famous reality show called **'Super Speaker'** which was conducted nationwide, and she finally was awarded as among **'Top 100 Motivational Speakers of India'**. Her philosophy of utilizing ones hidden potential to the fullest has always driven her to take that unknown new path and then excel in that area.

Notes

Notes

Dedicated To

Welcome, dear connoisseur, to the mesmerizing realm of perfumery, where fragrances dance and stories are told, where memories are captured and emotions unfold.

May my novel unfold like a delicate dance of aromatic notes, captivating the senses and whisking the reader away on a fragrant journey.

A homage to the craftsmanship and mystery, as, within each fragrance, a tale unfolds.

With the most exquisite olfactory salutations.

Publisher's Note

In the world of literature, there are books that entertain, books that inform, and then there are books that transcend mere storytelling to become immersive experiences. Vipul Suri's "Itr" undoubtedly falls into the latter category, offering readers an enchanting journey into the realm of perfume creation, and in doing so, unearths profound insights into the human soul.

At its essence, "Itr" is a story that revolves around the art of crafting scents, but it is so much more than that. It is a tale of self-discovery, identity, and the quest for purpose. Through the eyes and experiences of the protagonist, Vipul Suri, we are invited to delve deep into the captivating world of perfumery, where fragrances are not just chemical compositions but also vessels for memories, emotions, and stories.

The heart of "Itr" lies in Vipul Suri's personal journey, which beautifully intertwines with the creation of exquisite perfumes. As we follow him on his quest for the perfect fragrance, we also accompany him on a parallel journey of self-exploration and self-acceptance. This dual narrative structure adds layers of depth to the story, making it a poignant exploration of the interconnectedness between the creative process and one's own sense of identity.

The title itself, "Itr," is evocative. In many South Asian languages, "Itr" means perfume or essence, and it is often used in religious and spiritual contexts to represent the ethereal nature of life. In the book, "Itr" takes on this metaphorical significance, symbolizing not only the physical scents but also the intangible essence of life itself. Vipul Suri skillfully weaves this metaphor throughout the narrative, allowing readers to contemplate the profound connections between fragrance and the human experience.

As readers immerse themselves in the pages of "Itr," they are transported to a world where scent is more than a pleasant aroma; it is a means of communication, an art form, and a catalyst for introspection. Each perfume created in the story carries a piece of the protagonist's journey, mirroring his emotional state and personal growth. Through these fragrant creations, we witness the power of scent to evoke memories, stir emotions, and provoke introspection.

"Itr" invites readers to reflect on their own lives and experiences. It challenges us to consider the scents that have left indelible marks on our memories—the comforting aroma of a childhood home, the fragrance of a loved one, or the subtle scent of a significant moment. In doing so, the novel underscores the role of scent in our lives as a silent storyteller, a keeper of memories, and a bridge to our deepest emotions.

Beyond its thematic richness, "Itr" is beautifully written, with lyrical prose that captures the sensory experience of fragrance. Vipul Suri's descriptive talent allows readers to virtually smell the scents he describes, creating an immersive reading experience that stimulates the senses and ignites the imagination.

In conclusion, "Itr" by Vipul Suri is not just a book; it is a sensory and emotional journey that lingers long after the final page. It is a testament to the transformative power of fragrance and its metaphorical connection to life itself. For those who appreciate the art of scent and the intricate web of memories and emotions it weaves, "Itr" is a must-read. It is a reminder that, like perfume, life is a blend of various experiences, each contributing to the unique fragrance of our existence.

Acknowledgment

As I settle into the act of transcribing these sentiments of appreciation, my heart burgeons with a volley of emotions that mere words, in their limited capacity, can scarcely capture. The arduous voyage of sculpting this literary masterpiece has been a testament to my lifelong devotion, a magnificent tapestry closely linked with the essence of numerous souls who have graced my existence, leaving lasting impressions both profound and delicate. I humbly express my profound gratitude to each and every one of you.

In the vast landscape of my creative journey, there exists a guiding light that has illuminated the path with wisdom, encouragement, and unwavering belief. As I stand on the threshold of presenting my novel to the world, I am compelled to express my deepest gratitude to the individual who has been not only a mentor but also a beacon of inspiration – my revered guru.

How can words encapsulate the profound impact you have had on my life and the creation of this novel? Your presence in my journey has been nothing short of transformative, and your guidance has been a gentle but firm hand that sculpted my thoughts, nurtured my creativity, and emboldened me to embark on this literary odyssey.

Your wisdom extends far beyond the realm of technicalities; you have imparted life lessons that are interwoven with the narrative itself. The resilience, patience, and commitment you embody have become the underlying themes of this novel, a testament to the values you have instilled in me through your teachings. As I wrote about characters navigating their own struggles and triumphs, I often found myself drawing parallels to the journey you have guided me through.

In the quiet moments of uncertainty, you were the voice that whispered encouragement and the embodiment of unyielding faith in my abilities. Your words have echoed in my mind during the late nights and early mornings when the words flowed effortlessly, and also during the moments of doubt when the blank page seemed insurmountable. You have taught me that writing is not just about words on a page, but about connecting with the deepest parts of ourselves and sharing those vulnerabilities with the world.

Beyond your role as a mentor, you have been a cherished friend and confidant. Our discussions about literature, life, and the intricacies of the human experience have enriched my understanding and have been instrumental in shaping the themes of this novel. Your presence has been a constant reminder that creative endeavors are not solitary pursuits but collaborative efforts that are strengthened by the bonds we form along the way.

As I dedicate this novel to you, my guru, I am reminded of the words of gratitude exchanged between mentor and disciple for generations. But even those words feel insufficient when expressing the depth of my appreciation for all that you have done. This novel stands as a testament to the transformative power of your guidance, the profound influence of your insights, and the enduring warmth of your support.

I must express my deepest gratitude to my beloved family, for they are the foundation upon which my journey has been built. Their unwavering support and boundless encouragement have been the guiding lights that have illuminated my path, propelling me forward in my endeavors. My father, Mr. Rakesh Suri's unwavering faith in my abilities, even in the face of uncertainty, has served as the propelling motivation that has propelled this literary masterpiece forward. To my mother , I am forever indebted to the unwavering support and the selfless acts of sacrifice you have made, which have paved the way for me to embark upon this literary journey. It is upon the bedrock of your constant reassurance and the nurturing environment you have cultivated that this book finds its firm footing.

To my dearest and cherished spouse, whose constant presence has been a beacon of solace amidst the tumultuous nights, the relentless grip of writer's block, and the ceaseless iterations that have consumed my very being, I am compelled to express my profound gratitude for your boundless patience and empathetic comprehension. Indeed, it is your unwavering support that has breathed life into my weary soul, sustaining me through the arduous journey of creation. The unshakeable belief you have in me, coupled with your candid critique, has served as a luminous beacon, guiding me through the intricate maze of literature.

To my beloved daughters, you are the radiant stars that guided me through the realms of imagination, and your unwavering love has infused every word of this novel. Your laughter and wisdom inspired characters, your resilience painted landscapes, and your unwavering support breathed life into each page. This journey was woven with your encouragement, patience, and the warmth of our shared moments. As you read these lines, know that you're the beating heart of these words. My dedication to you is etched within these pages, forever a testament to the bond that fueled this creation

I am indebted to my dear friends, both longstanding and newfound, who have graciously bestowed upon me a haven of mirth, respite, and enlightenment. The immeasurable value of your receptiveness to my musings, your willingness to reciprocate with your own narratives, and your role as a sounding board for my contemplations cannot be overstated.

The realization of this novel's utmost potential owes its profound gratitude to the invaluable guidance bestowed upon it by my esteemed mentors and diligent beta readers. The invaluable contributions of their insights, astute suggestions, and thoughtful constructive criticisms have indelibly shaped and refined this manuscript, ultimately bringing it to its exquisite final form. The profound impact of your expertise and benevolence, as you graciously bestow upon me the gift of your time, cannot be overstated. It is through your invaluable guidance and support that my journey as a writer has been molded and refined.

A sincere and profound acknowledgement is also extended to the diverse array of professionals who graciously contributed their invaluable expertise to this valuable task. The invaluable insights bestowed upon me by the esteemed experts, the diligent researchers who graciously attended to my inquiries, and the fastidious editors who painstakingly scrutinized every aspect of the manuscript – it is with deep gratitude that I acknowledge the profound impact your contributions have had on enhancing the caliber of this endeavor.

I am filled with immense gratitude towards the communities that have warmly embraced me, both in the digital realm and in the physical world. These havens, where literature is celebrated and cherished, have provided me with a sanctuary to engage in profound discussions about writing techniques and the intricacies of storytelling. The profound sense of fellowship that has been demonstrated by your esteemed presence has illuminated the truth that the art of writing is not a solitary pursuit, but rather a magnificent collaborative endeavor that effortlessly transcends the limits of borders and boundaries.

In the realm of literature, it is an undeniable truth that a writer's journey is not a solitary one. Indeed, it is the unwavering support and tireless efforts of a dedicated team that propels an author forward, guiding them through the labyrinthine paths of their creative endeavors. In this regard, I consider myself immensely fortunate, for I have been blessed with a team that has stood steadfastly by my side, accompanying me on every stride of this literary odyssey. To the diligent agents, astute publicists, visionary designers, and all those unsung heroes who have toiled ceaselessly in the shadows, your unwavering commitment has metamorphosed mere words into a palpable masterpiece of artistry.

At long last, I humbly express my profound gratitude to the esteemed readers who are poised to embark upon this captivating literary odyssey. The profound gratitude I feel for your eagerness to delve into the lives of my characters and fully immerse yourselves in their intricately woven world is a humble offering that stirs within me a potent blend of exhilaration and eager anticipation.

Ultimately, a novel transcends the mere accumulation of its pages, for it embodies a profound contemplation of the elaborate tapestry of human existence, linked with a multitude of connections that define our very being. Every individual mentioned within these pages, and the countless others whose names remain unspoken, has bestowed upon this tapestry of appreciation a single stroke of their brush. As I bestow upon the world this literary opus, I do so with a profound understanding that its genesis transcends the boundaries of my individuality, for it is a manifestation woven intricately from the collective fabric of shared encounters, shared aspirations, and shared encouragement.

Yours Faithfully
Vipul Suri

Itr: A Fragrant Odyssey

Greetings.

I am Vipul, a married Punjabi gentleman residing in the city of Lucknow. My name often proves to be a challenge for others to pronounce, resulting in a curious tendency for them to refer to me as SURI. Behold the tale of my awakening to the realization that I am blessed with the privilege of being a part of the wonderful world of fragrances.

The book's title derives from a common exchange that served as a customary salutation upon one's return to their hometown. The words were spoken in a hushed tone, a gesture that conveyed not only kindness but also a genuine curiosity about the appearance of others, thereby fostering a sense of intimacy and individuality. It was my impression that certain individuals harbor a covert yearning to perceive the aroma emanating from another individual, in order to subjectively find their own fondness.

One Chapter Ends, Another Begins

In the year 1999, a milestone was reached as I completed my high school education and entered adulthood at the age of 18. With the collusion of these two transformative experiences, I was transported to a realm brimming with ambition, enlightenment, companionship, revelry, and obligations. As the seasons changed, it was time to bid farewell to the familiar faces of classmates, childhood friends, and playground acquaintances. The initial veracity that confronts you upon awakening to your senses is that of disconnection. The experience was a sharp and intense sensation.

My olfactory memory effortlessly retrieves the various scents that diffused throughout my former educational institution, even on a subconscious level. As a novice perfumer, I must say that the scent of the library has always captivated my olfactory senses. Upon entering a library, one is enveloped by a bouquet of blooming letters, each with its own unique signature scent of inky notes and a hint of leathery undertones from their bindings. Furthermore, each book possesses a unique and distinct fragrance. As you gently extract one of the books from the shelf, a smooth and earthy aroma envelops your senses, reminiscent of velvet and wood. The vintage scents possess a rich and intense aroma that immediately captivates the senses upon unveiling. One can detect hints of amber, salt, and water, while the newer, popular fragrances exude a fresh and crisp benzene scent. This fragrance presents itself with a distinct character, reminiscent of a well-aged scent or a newly acquired one. The former exudes a rich and robust aroma that lingers in the air upon opening, while the latter boasts a crisp and invigorating scent that awakens the senses. The aroma is the essence that lingers long after the encounter; refrain from making hasty conclusions based on appearances. The olfactory atmosphere is saturated with the fragrance of clusters of unprocessed cotton.

At the next destination, the biology laboratory, oh my, what an experience it was. A bold and complex aroma, featuring animalic and etheric nuances intertwined with hints of simmered green foliage. As you approach it, its essence becomes more and more apparent to your senses.

Beyond the next 100 steps lies the chemistry lab, where fragrant concoctions await. The atmosphere was a symphony of intoxicating scents, blending aldehydic, aromatic, sulfurous, metallic, and salty notes. I relished my time there and was captivated by the fragrant nuances on encountering a diverse array of both liquid and solid elements, even though some expectations were not met. To my nose, the art of perfumery demands the harmonious blending of a variety of intricate and exotic ingredients, each with its own unique character. A single misstep in this delicate dance can lead to a less than satisfactory outcome, requiring the perfumer to refine their formula until it achieves the desired effect. Perhaps that was Pita Ji's intent when he asked me to keep up my education and concentrate on scientific topics.

Our humble eatery was positioned at the edge of our front garden. The day was filled with the savory aroma of burgers and frankies, complemented by the refreshing scent of cold drinks. In that corner, a delightful scent lingered, which I named Gusto. It was a harmonious blend of warm bread, sizzling eggs, pungent onions, and tangy tomato sauce. An enigmatic blend of diverse scent molecules captivates the senses, and to indulge in this delicacy, one must either keep it clandestine or foster intimate connections with those commemorating a birthday.

During that period, I found myself exceptionally drawn to. A popular Fougere, elevated with zesty notes of lemon and bergamot, leading to a delightful sweet woody scent featuring a captivating blend of invigorating spices and a commanding aromatic essence, this fragrance boasts a resolute and powerful character. Its audacious undertones reveal a velvety powdery allure, while the mossy impressions add a touch of sophistication and intrigue. As a Like a budding artisan in the realm of fragrance creation, when I reminisce about my school days, my mind is filled with a plethora of memories that evoke a range of emotions, leaving a lingering impression on my senses. The exertion will inevitably cause you to lose your breath soon. The longing to reunite with dear friends and reminisce about cherished memories is a fragrance that lingers in my heart. Crossroads evoked a certain essence. The anticipation built as we eagerly awaited its arrival, the passing of an entire year only adding to the excitement. In my fledgling journey as a perfumer, I recall a time when I was a student at a boys' school and took part in a competitive event. It was during this time that I formed a new friendship and discovered a fondness for cuddling. The allure of popularity and fame is often associated with participation in trendy events, charming esthetics, or a robust physique. Regrettably, these traits eluded me, though several of my acquaintances possessed them effortlessly.

After much contemplation, the moment had arrived to choose a path for graduate studies. The revelation was a scent I had never encountered, but now it is unmistakable.

To create a captivating scent, one must carefully consider each note in advance, lest the final product falls flat and disappoint the senses. The essence of the world around you poses a familiar inquiry: what shall you do, and where shall you venture? The whys cascade upon you, with no definitive response. In perfume creation, some fragrances are carefully crafted with a clear vision from the start, while others rely on the blending of various notes to create a harmonious scent. Pita Ji's words were a fragrant inspiration that lingered with me, leading me to pursue the art of pharmaceutical sciences.

The scent of my rescue lingered delicately, as if it had been carefully crafted and timed to perfection. Every option has its own unique advantages and disadvantages. As I couldn't return to my abode, I chose Ooty as my ultimate destination.

Honestly, that name is not within my olfactory repertoire. In the absence of the internet, our olfactory inspiration was solely derived from the printed word and the individuals in our immediate surroundings.

The Genesis

In the fragrant month of June, I discovered myself amidst the captivating essence of Ooty. I had chosen to embark on a journey to master the art of pharmaceutical sciences.

To truly understand the intricacies of natural and synthetic scents, as well as the art of blending them, one must delve into the chemistry behind them. It is also crucial to become well-versed in product formulation and adhere to the scientific protocols and research standards outlined in literature. Mastery of these topics is essential for any aspiring perfumer.

To embark on the journey of perfumery, one may opt to pursue excellence in chemistry or arts and psychology. As a perfumer, your journey will involve working with a variety of aromatic chemicals and natural ingredients, and the knowledge of science will be a valuable aid.

The time I spent there has allowed me to confidently declare Ooty as one of the most visually stunning hill stations I have ever had the pleasure of visiting. The journey to reach the Valley of Ooty was a long and winding one, taking us on a 48-hour train ride, followed by a 3.5-hour road bus journey from the nearest station. This odyssey was a fragrant one, but the final essence was truly exquisite.

A select few olfactory nuances will forever be etched in my memory. The fragrance of my hometown lingers in the north, while Ooty's aroma wafts from the south. As one journeys from one realm to another, the very essence of the surroundings transforms, including the fragrances that permeate the atmosphere. Every sense is imbued with the essence of this transformation.

I cite, as an example, the aromatic foliage of curry leaves, belonging to the family Rutaceae, a leaf that was previously unknown to me until that moment. Upon extraction, it emanates a zesty citrus top note intertwined with a crisp green body. Upon crushing, it reveals a robust amber woody base note. This petite leaf boasts an oval shape and a lush, verdant hue. This leaf is truly a complex and aromatic creation by nature itself. Unexpectedly, it has a more delightful flavor when employed during the chilling procedure. The aromatic essence of curry leaves graced every dish that caught my attention. The inherent naturalness of this ingredient imbues it with a unique quality that elevates it to the forefront of any culinary creation. The dish is not overpowered, but rather enhanced by a subtle twist that adds to its appeal. A highly versatile element that not only enhances the esthetic appeal but also imparts a unique flavor to various dishes, including aromatic rice infused with tangy curd and zesty lemon, flavorful sambar, flaky kuttu paratha, spiced porial, succulent chicken chettinad, and a variety of other delectable dishes. In my olfactory exploration, I dared to blend the sweet essence of honey and tangy notes of lemon with the boldness of brandy, vodka, and rum. To add a touch of exoticism, I infused a hint of curry leaf and finished with a sparkling touch of Fizz. The result was a daring concoction I named Macha.

Ooty is reminiscent of the invigorating scent of wintergreen. The crisp air of Ooty's high altitude mingled with the constant rainfall, creating a unique and refreshing scent that permeated the city year-round. As the rain falls, the soul notes of the earth ascend carrying with them the earthy, green, and musty scents. These notes blend with the aromatic green wintergreen, creating a natural accord that is rich and weighty.

The crisp, wintry breeze carries the invigorating essence of wintergreen, diffusing its verdant aroma throughout the hillside, imparting a soothing and revitalizing ambiance. Upon my initial visit to a new spa, I detected a distinct fragrance that exuded an innate understanding of the art of relaxation. Allow me to briefly touch on the topic of well-being: infuse the winter green leaves in boiling water and savor the aromatic steam to alleviate nasal congestion. The aromatic overtones of winter green really offer a sense of tranquilly, and it takes me back to many occasions in childhood when my mother gently applied an infusion of this oil on my back and chest before putting me to sleep to clear my nasal congestion. This would help me get off to a good night's sleep. Some scents can transport people to the past, while others can take them into the future.

The temples in my hometown exude a distinct aroma of architectural style, unlike the ones I encountered in Ooty. As an aspiring perfumer, from a young age, even though I couldn't fully understand the prayers, the subtle nuances and sensations that I experienced while visiting a temple left me with a feeling of divine grace.

Upon passing through the temple's entrance, a delicate aroma of sweet, warm, and starchy notes reminiscent of freshly cooked rice wafts through the air. The sweet, green notes of wet banana leaves blend harmoniously with these notes as boiling hot sambar is poured over them. As you perform this task, you are enveloped in the fragrance of the sanctuary. This blend, in my olfactory perception, produces a unique accord that is simultaneously deeply rooted in tradition and uncomplicated. As you approach the sculptures of the supreme deity, the heightened vibrations envelop your being, cleansing your soul with their powerful essence. As you delve deeper, a distinct and tranquil signature profile emerges, reminiscent of sacred spaces, exclusive to places of worship. A vibrant yellow bloom known as marigold lends its citrusy floral notes to a soulful bouquet, complemented by the lush, sweet, and verdant aroma of pristine white flowers. I sense the essence of jasmine emanating from your being, gracefully blending into the luminous beige aura of sandalwood. As you saunter through the aisle towards the exit, the alluring essence of benzoin enhances the ambiance of vitality.

Upon your departure, the lingering aroma of musky, ambery, and dusty charcoal sticks serves as a signature, affirming your encounter with the divine.

Jasmine, as a fragrance, is undoubtedly a familiar one to all of us. I stumbled upon the realization that the whiteness in Ooty was notably distinct from that of my hometown, and it exuded a greater sense of reverence. The fragrance had always been associated with auspicious occasions and sacred places; yet in Ooty, it was incorporated into the town's ambiance. The delicate jasmine garlands adorning the tresses of ladies can be elegantly arranged. Throughout the day, the wreath's fragrance lingered in the air.

As a nose, one can discern the scent of jasmine in the air, and yet the fragrance of a passing woman catches the attention with its sweet, floral, and green notes. The scent of jasmine possesses a distinct and recognizable signature. A well-known individual exudes a delightful and charming aura, adorned in a flawless white saree paired with a lime green blouse. Ah, the jasmine flower, a delicate beauty that only reveals its true essence at night! It is during midday that we carefully pluck this precious bloom, knowing that its full potential can only be unlocked through the art of oil extraction.

Ah, coffee. Its cultural significance is as intriguing as its warm and invigorating aroma. The essence of this culture was unmistakable in Ooty, as the city boasted a plethora of cafes reminiscent of the tea kiosks found in our hometown. The essence of Ooty's culture is intertwined with the aromatic tea that is grown in the Nilgiris Valley, where Ooty is nestled. The setting of my alma mater was atop Elk Hill, in close proximity to the old HMT factory.

During my entire five-year tenure as a student, I resided in the college hostel. At the break of dawn, before the ritualistic meal, we would commence our day with a fragrant cup of coffee. At the early hours of the day, one can prepare a rich and invigorating coffee for personal enjoyment. A robust steel vessel, holding 10 liters of freshly brewed filter coffee, was positioned by the responsible individuals amidst the chaos. As you pour the coffee into your vessel of choice, take a moment to inhale the rich, nutty aroma. Notice the notes of dark roast, nuttiness, and woody undertones. Allow the scent to awaken your senses and invigorate your mind. A harmonious blend of rich coffee, creamy milk, and sweet sugar was already prepared.

When coffee is blended with milk, it enhances the authentic nutty aroma. Adding sugar creates a harmonious balance, making it a delightful morning indulgence. To my nose, it evokes a delectable and nutty gourmand scent. The essence of coffee exudes a distinct aura. The olfactory notes evocative of coffee pervaded the entire storage space. In Ooty, one could indulge in the aroma of flavored coffee and tea. The memory of the chocolate tea and orange coffee lingers on in my senses.

Upon entering the enchanting realm of a luxurious perfume boutique, one is greeted by a captivating ambiance. A delightful interplay of scents dances in the air, captivating the senses. However, it is important to note that the presence of a coffee box, while alluring, may not provide an accurate olfactory backdrop for the meticulous evaluation of fragrances. The captivating essence of coffee entices the senses, evoking a revitalizing sensation while delicately vanishing with the perception of its scent. In order to truly immerse oneself in the olfactory experience, it is essential to engage in a delicate ritual. Begin by delicately grasping the fragrance-infused blotter, allowing it to rest gently between your fingertips. With a graceful motion, bring it closer to your nose, allowing the enchanting aroma to envelop your senses. As you inhale, savor the intricate layers of the fragrance, allowing each breath to reveal its nuanced complexities. Take a momentary pause, allowing the fragrance's unique signature to unfold before your discerning nose. Ah, the Cinnamon Forest. Its alluring aroma eluded me until my last year of undergraduate studies. In a remote setting, veiled from the sight of wandering travelers for motives that remain mysterious. Ah, cinnamon. A fascinating subject that I delved into during my study of pharmacognosy. Belonging to the Lauraceae family, its bioactives, polyphenols, and a variety of other chemical components play an important part in pharmaceuticals as well. The ingredient is widely employed in the creation of biryani and is, in fact, a fundamental element of every Indian household's spice blend. The wood chip's squill possesses a unique chemical composition also utilized as a remedy for various ailments. As time elapsed, I detected that it is also employed in baking. It has a dry, sweet, and woody note that, when chipped, reveals a potent and pungent sweetness, and when tasted, unveils an exquisite sweetness.

The fragrance possesses a sweet and warm essence. The art of flavoring chewing" paan "betel leaf, a prominent culinary industry in India, involves the exquisite use of cinnamon, a vital and noteworthy ingredient in the process. The sweetness of it is certainly alluring, but it's the woody undertones that truly shine, especially when paired with the deep notes of tobacco. And let's not forget its ability to stimulate saliva production, which keeps people coming back for more.

The fragrance is not only sweet, but also has a woody profile that shines through on the darker tobacco notes. The captivating realm of pharmacognosy has piqued my interest. The natural woody components, roots, leaves, seeds, and fruits all had distinct aroma profiles that were helpful in identifying and understanding their medicinal properties. A harmonious blend of warm cinnamon, spicy clove oil, aromatic cardamom, and zesty ginger, enhanced with a touch of sweet maltol and the alluring galaxolide. This fragrance is reminiscent of the beloved masala tea. For persistent cough, I suggest carrying a small chip of licorice and a small chip of cinnamon on your tongue to soothe your throat.

The intricacies of chemistry are fascinating, and my background in pharmaceutical sciences has provided me with valuable insights into the realms of cosmetics, perfumery, medicine, and research. I believe Pita ji would be proud of my understanding. The essence of pharmaceutical chemistry centered around the curative applications of chemistry, akin to the chemistry honors curriculum. Through my olfactory education, I have come to understand the nuances of aldehydes, ketones, amines, alcohols, and esters.

Pillars of Inspiration

How to become an expert in Perfumery?

In 2005, the poignant chapter of college life came to a close. A profound transformation in my existence took place. Through my experiences, I have come to appreciate the essence of self-reliance, fearlessness, hard work, and enjoyment. The essence of my youth was marked by a solitary existence, as few of my peers resided in the dormitory. Despite this, I embraced the opportunity to savor each moment, recognizing that this fleeting time would never be recaptured, and that I would ultimately navigate life's journey independently. The vivacity of my senior classmates surpassed that of my peers; thus, I gravitated towards their company. The fragrances of Lifebuoy soap, Sunsilk shampoo, Surf fabric detergent, Breeze soap, Mysore Sandal soap, Ponds cream, Clinic Plus shampoo, and Parachute hair oil, have seamlessly blended into my daily routine and personal aura.

The moment had arrived to craft a choice concerning the final segment of the learning journey. After careful consideration, I determined that my olfactory senses were best suited for the pursuit of a master's degree in pharmacy. The process of qualifying for a scholarship required numerous tests, the exact count of which eludes me. At this juncture, I realized that pursuing a master's degree in pharmacy would furnish me with robust groundwork in the art of perfumery, a domain that I aspired to venture into in the future.

The notion of master's degree programs in France never crossed my mind, as my focus was solely on the pharmaceutical industry. Destiny intervened, as I was all set to join a renowned pharmacy institution in India, but my father's acquaintances from India whispered something intriguing in his ear. Upon reviewing the course details, I observed that the venue is situated in Mumbai, a splendid location for pursuing undergraduate studies. The allure was so captivating that I elected to partake in this two-year program.

PGDPCM is an acronym for Post Graduate Diploma in Perfumery and Cosmetics Management, which entails a two-year exploration of perfumery in its most intimate form. Our batch's success has paved the way for many budding talents, and I am filled with pride.

In mid-2005, I embarked on a fragrant journey by enrolling in a class in Mumbai. The olfactory essence of Mumbai's atmosphere is truly distinctive. This fragrance evokes a complex blend of fame, opportunity, glamour, struggle, and dreams. As an aspiring perfumer, upon discovering the ubiquitous presence of the ocean's scent, one may come to appreciate its allure. The salty aroma is unmistakable. It was the commencement of my olfactory odyssey to unearth my true essence, or rather, my innermost ardor for the art of perfumery. In this environment, the possibilities are endless. One must simply challenge themselves and apply ample dedication to achieve greatness. To become a perfumer, it demands much from you, yet it never withholds its finest offerings.

The essence of Mumbai's diverse memories and moments, its fragrance journey, commences with the captivating first impressions of Mumbai, unfolding at the bustling Dadar railway station. Dadar's train station emanates a familiar aroma common to other bustling cities in India, yet it possesses unique olfactory characteristics that are unmistakably its own, including the aromatic missal pav, savory vada pav, flavorful pav bhaji, and fragrant cutting chai. The essence of being a true Mumbaikar lies in savoring these delectable specialties. This is not just a simple bite; rather, it is a full course. The aroma of midday sustenance varies, with some indulging in a traditional lunch, while others savor the delicate notes of a mid-morning brunch.

To my nose, vada pav is a harmonious blend of notes, featuring a spicy, starchy, green, and salty heart nestled within a crispy wheat shell. The fragrance is accented with sharp, pungent sparks and a hint of sulfur, all captured in a soft, musky layer with a touch of balsamic. The presentation is reminiscent of an old amber crushed sheet.

The Mumbai rains possess a distinct character that sets them apart from the Ooty rains. While Ooty experiences rainfall all year, Mumbai's rainfall is limited to the months of June to August. Nevertheless, the Mumbai rains exude a cinematic quality rather than a scenic one. A multitude of aromatic notes waft gracefully in every direction. If you breathe in the air at Juhu Beach, for instance, you will perceive a distinct aroma compared to standing at a railway station, and Lonavala will be the perfect finishing touch. Mumbai's rain is a multi-hued symphony of 50 distinct colors. In Juhu, the powdery earth notes mingle with the wet earth and salty sea notes, while warm tomato fumes interrupt the rain's serenity. The tomato notes evolve into a spicy freshness, adding sultriness to the moment. As you release your emotional thoughts, the desire for spicy, sweet, and hot tea is revealed.

Bollywood, a genre that evades easy definition. The olfactory notes linked with Bollywood possess a unique identity of their own. Regrettably, it has not been crafted yet, but maybe we could endeavor to create it. This fragrance is a complex and uniquely crafted scent, a rich and complex blend of amber, opoponax, smoky tobacco, and resinous whisky, harmoniously balanced with the cool and refreshing essence of watery peony and zesty lemon, all carefully crafted and stored in a luxurious leather bottle, adorned with a stunning diamond.

Ah, ambrox, patchouli, labdanum, cade, calone, lemon, and other such exquisite ingredients.

Upon my initial arrival at the university, I detected a plethora of new acquaintances, each with their own unique scent. With each step, I was enveloped in the alluring essence of their presence. My treasured friends Gopal and Jinesh had mastered the technical nuances of this field and commenced the creative process well before I did. It is intriguing that in the past, perfumery did not pique the interest of many individuals. However, presently, over 90% of our batch is utilized in the art of fragrance creation.

The allure of perfumery and crafting scents is undeniable. Once you begin, it becomes a lifelong passion that transcends time. The art lies in the act of smelling and persisting until you can recognize, without any visual aid, at least three hundred distinct ingredients. Only then can the true artistry commence. The essence lies in the olfactory experience. Upon my olfactory analysis, the initial note that graced my senses was that of phenyl ethyl alcohol. Its aroma evoked a verdant hue and the delicate texture of blooming Rose petals. My discerning nose detected its presence at a concentration of 10 percent. The essence of a rose is a crucial element, as my friend informed me. As an aspiring fragrance expert, you know that the art of fragrance creation is shrouded in secrecy, and one must earn their knowledge through personal experience. The secrets of this exquisite craft are fiercely guarded, for it is not only a thing of beauty, but also a source of great wealth. In 2004, our olfactory library was graced with a select few tomes, including perfumery bibles from great authors, including Steffen Arcatander, William A. Poucher, and Ernest Guenther. These precious volumes provided us with indisputable and exquisitely precise knowledge. I immerse myself in literature to fully absorb the knowledge within. In the early stages of your fragrance journey, the vast realm of knowledge may appear to dissipate, much like the evaporation of delicate aromatic molecules. For fragrance creation is an art form that demands extensive practice and dedication. Perfumery may not have initially piqued my interest, but true art is subjective and personal, evoking unexpected emotions and sensations. Upon further reflection, I came to the profound realization that the enchanting encounter with fragrance is an utterly distinctive and personal journey for every individual.

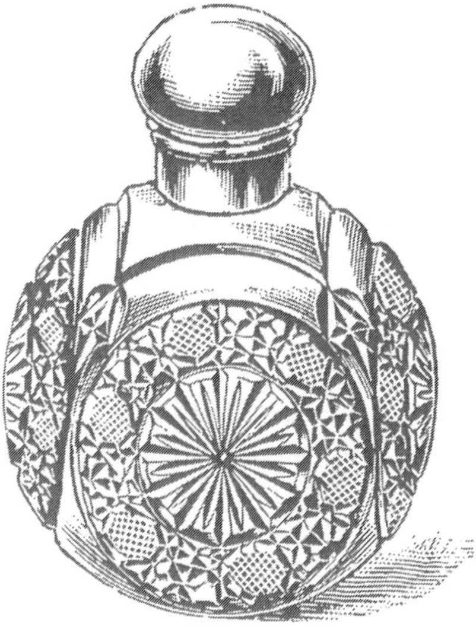

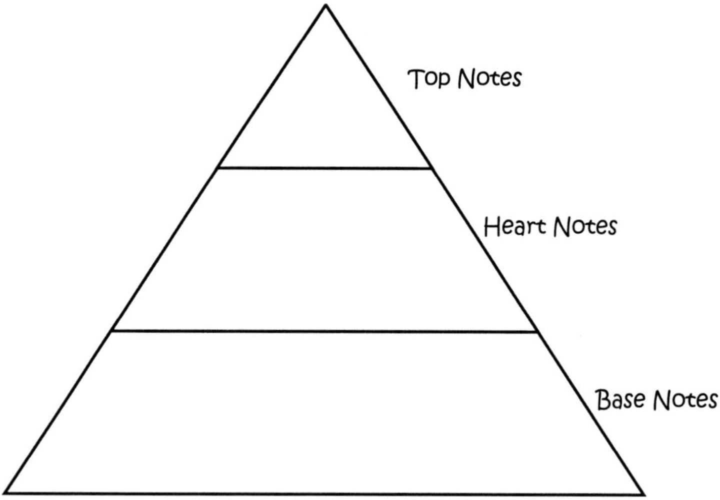
Top Notes
Heart Notes
Base Notes

Harmonizing with Solitude:

How to Study Perfumery?

The art of perfume-making involves a plethora of ingredients that can be blended in endless ways to create a unique and captivating scent. As an aspiring perfumer, I had the freedom to experiment and craft a fragrance that is truly one-of-a-kind.

To truly comprehend perfumery, one must possess a deep understanding of its components, referred to as ingredients. Today, one can explore myriad fragrant gems in diverse shapes and sizes. To truly understand them, one must spend time alone with them in a structured manner. To thrive in the alluring realm of fragrances, one must memorize each scent, record their observations, and nurture their imaginative faculties.

The cultivation of one's sense of smell is of utmost significance and must never be disregarded or disrupted. As fragrance experts, we abide by a strict regimen of daily olfactory training to hone our expertise in the art of fragrance composition. To this end, we dedicate a half-hour each day to this exercise, approaching it with a competitive zeal that fuels our passion for the craft.

It must be reiterated that no "nose" can be deemed superior to another, and it is solely a matter of olfactory recollection for which daily practice is not only required, but essential.

The olfactory sense is the sole instrument of the perfumer. A skilled perfumer knows that possessing a refined sense of smell, along with a remarkable olfactory recollection, is merely the foundation for crafting exceptional fragrances. A skilled perfumer, or "nose," possesses the ability to discern between a pure and adulterated product as well as differentiate between concentrations of similar ingredients. Although I have some experience, I still consider myself nascent compared to the seasoned "noses".

As I embark on my journey, I am eager to divulge some of the initial notes that have caught my attention. Through careful observation and study, I have familiarized myself with these scents and allowed them to permeate my senses.

The art of perfumery classifies fragrance components into two distinct categories: naturals and synthetics. The term "synthetic," however, could potentially convey an inaccurate perception to certain individuals. These are exquisite aromatic molecules crafted to emulate the alluring scents of rare botanicals that are unattainable through traditional extraction methods.

As a perfumer, one must understand the intricacies of fragrance evaluation and be knowledgeable about the nuances of scent. Who, then, is the expert on fragrance evaluation. The essence of my craft may be familiar to most, yet I've encountered countless individuals who fail to grasp the intricacies of my profession. The scent eluded even my own senses. I endeavor to elucidate it to them in a manner that is comprehensible by stating that I am a perfumer. As a perfumer, describing my workplace can be a complex task when asked about the company I am affiliated with. To my olfactory senses, a perfumer is a skilled artisan who crafts a symphony of scents, delicately blending various ingredients to achieve a harmonious balance that exudes pure beauty. The exquisite blend is carefully crafted and presented to our esteemed clientele as a fragrance. In my past, I have had the pleasure of embodying the roles of both a perfumer and a perfume evaluator. As a perfumer, I believe that a perfume evaluator plays a crucial role in the creative process. They are not just reviewers, but empathetic individuals who assist us in crafting a scent that resonates with different cultures and tells a unique story. Ultimately, our goal is to fulfil the emotional desires of our customers through our fragrances. In the world of fragrance, the harmonious blend of these two elements forms the very essence of a perfume's being.

In the initial phase of this olfactory expedition, your sole mission is to persistently explore and experience the diverse elements that constitute the foundation of this aromatic odyssey. Before indulging in the olfactory experience, one must ensure that all necessary safety measures are taken into account, as this is a continuous endeavor. To preserve the intricate essence of the ingredient, one must repeatedly revisit the ingredients, whether in a haphazard manner or in a specific order. As a beginner, one must not only rely on their sense of smell, but also consult technical literature while evaluating ingredients. Later, one embarks on a journey of assessing the components.

In this chapter, I shall delve into some of my cherished ingredients, a few of which I had the privilege of experiencing in their purest form. My father, an artist in his own right, would often incorporate these attars and extracts into his creations in his laboratory. One should allow the ingredient to reveal its essence, rather than imposing preconceived notions that may obscure its inherent beauty.

Families, specifically "olfactive families," are the first phrase used in perfumery. The phrase is used to group distinct scents from either a completed perfume or its ingredients into specific families. While some perfumers have their own clearly defined families to make comprehension easier, there are a few standard ones that one should never forget. The strategy is to group ingredients and fragrances into the main, secondary, and tertiary families because they all have different nuances. This makes them easier to map and reduces complexity. There are no restrictions on placing them in these families; one is allowed to do so according to how they perceive and interact with them. You must be asking why there are just three families, as opposed to four or more. The primary family is to classify it under the umbrella family first, then the underlying note or smell that you initially detect, and finally, as you dig deeper into understanding of the very ingredient or perfume, you will find the unique profile that further distinguishes it from others in the same family. We occasionally add a fourth level, which may be an attribute, or a sentiment related to the third. In summary, grouping odors into families not only improves the ability to differentiate between them but also makes it easier to remember, describe, and apply them in creations. Therefore, learning about families must be the first step. In addition, when the field of perfumery develops further, new olfactory families may appear, including some of the key families one must learn, as below, to start with.

Aromatic: Aromatic scents include lavender, sage, and rosemary, among other herbal and/or spicy undertones.

Aquatic: Fragrances that evoke the aroma of the ocean or water are referred to as aquatic and frequently contain marine notes and aquatic botanicals.

Citrus: Fragrances that are light, fresh, and crisp and that include notes of citrus, green leaves, and zest.

Floral: Rose, jasmine, violet, and other fresh flowers are some of the notes that are included in such fragrances.

Fruity: Fragrances which bring lushy sweet and juicy notes of exotic fruits such as apples, peaches, raspberries, and other similar fruits.

Green: The olfactory family of green contains scents that resemble the aromas of grass, green leaves and plants.

Musky: The olfactory group known as "musky" includes scents that have a sensual, warm, and animalistic aroma.

Woody: Perfumes which have notes of different kinds of wood, including vetiver, cedar, and sandalwood.

Amber: The aromas of amber, vanilla, and labdanum make up the warm and opulent fragrance category known as "amber." Many people describe amber smells as having a warm, comforting character and being woody, resinous, and just a little bit sweet.

Fougere: In perfumery, the olfactory family of Fougère (pronounced "foo-jair") is distinguished by a blend of lavender, oakmoss, and coumarin. In 1882, Houbigant created this olfactory family with the production of Fougère Royale, often regarded as the first modern fragrance.

Chypre: a sophisticated aroma that combines floral, woodsy, and mossy elements, frequently with bergamot, oakmoss, and patchouli.

Gourmand: Fragrances with sweet and savory undertones, such as caramel, chocolate, and vanilla.

Aldehydic: Aldehydes are aromatic molecules that give off a distinctive and potent scent, and the term "aldehydic" describes scents that include a substantial amount of them. The famous scent Chanel No. 5, which blends aldehydes with floral notes, and Guerlain's Shalimar, which combines aldehydes with vanilla and exotic spices, are two examples of fragrances from the aldehydic family.

Animalic: Fragrances that resemble the smell of animal products or bodily secretions, such as musk, civet, and castoreum, belong to the olfactory family known as animalic.

Leathery: Leather-scented fragrances, frequently paired with additional elements like tobacco and spices. Reminiscent of suede.

I meticulously recorded all my olfactory impressions in a dedicated journal, which I would occasionally consult. Over time, it became second nature to commit them to memory. Taking notes is an essential practice, especially in the early stages of your craft, and even as you continue to develop as an artist.

The Scent of Ingredients

How to Smell Ingredients?

The initial ritual of this olfactory journey involves immersing oneself in the art of discerning and appraising various aromatic constituents. Through the depths of my aromatic education, I have come to discover a wealth of knowledge, unveiling the intricacies of this captivating art form. Indulging in the following guidelines will enable you to effectively appreciate the olfactory essence of perfume upon a delicate blotter. Pick a blotter strip or testing paper that is spotlessly clean. You should steer clear of utilizing paper that has a potent odor or residue from other scents.

Holding the bottle a few inches away from the blotter strip and spraying the fragrance onto it will prevent the paper from becoming too saturated. You might also use a pipette or a dropper to put a drop of perfume on the blotter instead.

Before you smell the fragrance, give the blotter strip a few seconds to absorb the scent and allow it to settle. This will allow the smell to evolve over time and expose the various notes that it contains.

Keep the blotter strip a couple of inches away from your nose. This distance is close enough for you to detect the scent, but it is not so close that it will overpower your senses.

Take a few long breaths through your nose, inhaling the scent fully and allowing it to permeate your other senses as well. You can also disseminate the fragrance and enjoy the many levels of it by gently waving the blotter strip in front of your nose.

Make a mental note of the many notes that the scent possesses, such as the top notes (which create the first impression), the middle notes (which create the heart of the smell), and the base notes (which create the impression that lasts the longest). Try smelling the blotter strip once more after some time has passed to observe how the scent shifts over the course of the experiment.

It is important to remember to smell perfumes on your skin as well, as body chemistry can cause smells to smell different on various people. In general, sniffing perfume on a blotter strip is an amazing approach to test and experience different smells and to select scents that you prefer. You can test and experience different perfumes.

The initiation of a novice in the art of perfumery must commence with the olfactory examination of all fragrant substances, whether they be of natural or synthetic origin. In order to facilitate such a study, the beginner will first be given to smell contrasting odors, and later materials belonging to a certain odor "family". In other spheres, I have been presented with two tables pertaining to the study of scents, in accordance with specific criteria. Learning to smell on smelling strips, to identify and to distinguish from one another all odorous materials, the beginner will soon notice that the odor of the products changes with time, that the rate of evaporation is not the same for all products.

The subsequent phase entails establishing a categorization of fragrant substances based on their evaporation rate.

Very volatile products lacking tenacity are top notes.

Middle notes are of intermediate volatility and tenacity modifiers.

Fragrances with a low evaporation rate and long-lasting scent are base notes.

As the name suggests, the base notes are the foundation of the fragrance, providing a long-lasting and essential character to the perfume. The success of the scent relies heavily on these notes, which will linger for hours on end.

Those with a keen understanding of perfume materials know that fragrances with low volatility and high tenacity, such as vetiver, oak moss, patchouli, and methyl ionone, may emit an unpleasant odor when first applied to smelling strips. However, as they evaporate, their scent transforms into something truly exceptional. The utilization of intermediate volatility and tenacity modifiers is essential to transform the base notes' unpleasant top note.

Symphony with Naturals

How to Start learning the Natural Ingredients ?

The art of discovering natural perfume ingredients is truly captivating, igniting the imagination and expanding olfactory horizons. The diverse range of botanicals, including plants, trees, and flowers, offer a unique scent profile and therapeutic benefits that are utilized in perfumery.

Every element possesses a unique personality that contributes to the blend, and when combined, they can be used to tell a story, evoke a feeling, or evoke cherished reminiscences. The use of natural ingredients enables the creation of fragrances that are not only visually appealing but also pleasing to the senses of the wearer.

Crafting fragrances using natural materials is a true art. It requires a keen sense of exploration to uncover new possibilities, a creative touch to blend them in unique combinations, and a delicate balance to evoke profound emotions through scent. Ah, the nuances of scent, the alchemy of fragrance, and the artistry of blending - all essential knowledge for crafting a bespoke perfume.

Patchouli: Woody

This ingredient is undoubtedly cherished by perfumers all around the world. This leafy scent is categorized as woody due to its inherent qualities. In my olfactory opinion, no composition can truly be considered complete without the addition of the rich and earthy aroma of patchouli. In my olfactory recollection, I recall a rich, deep brownish-green elixir that exuded a sense of sophistication and warmth. It was as if it were dressed in luxurious brown linens with a hint of green, and its hair was impeccably shiny. The aroma was completed by the subtle presence of a Cuban cigar.

At varying dilutions, it reveals its diverse hues to me. At 1% concentration, it evokes the scent of a freshly picked Rooty herb. When diluted to 10%, it transforms into a refreshing aroma of suede wood. And, at 50%, it exudes a captivating essence of sultry amber. Ah, Pandari, a name that evokes the exotic beauty of India. It is said to be the Hindi name for patchouli, a fragrant plant with a long history in perfumery. The extensive utilization of this ingredient has been discovered in classic fragrances. Patchouli is a beloved scent for many. This fragrance exudes an enigmatic aura of uncharted subtleties that captivates perfumers worldwide, beckoning them to delve deeper into its allure. A certain ingredient, when used in excess, creates an irresistible urge to wear it repeatedly. Today, Indonesia is the world's foremost supplier for Patchouli.

My first accord with patchouli. Patchouli – 1 gm, Labdanum – 0.5 gm, Geranium – 0.5 gm, Sandalwood – 1 gm.

Vetiver: Woody

In my olfactory memory, this fragrance is reminiscent of Khus, a beloved scent from my hometown. This scent evokes a plethora of nostalgic childhood memories. This botanical specimen is a root, and yet, its classification is that of a woody nature. A stunning creation has emerged, a sofa adorned in lush bottle green velvets and accented with warm wood brown cushions, exuding a richly sweet and fresh aroma.

The unique quality of vetiver lies in its inherent sweetness. At a mere 1% dilution, one can detect a subtle yet alluring sweetness. However, as the concentration increases to 10% and beyond, the fragrance takes on a more luxurious and velvety suede quality. At higher dilutions, the scent becomes even more captivating with a sweet and damp woody essence. This exquisite extract begins as a luscious green liquid and evolves into a rich brown hue as it matures. This creation possesses a certain enchantment. With a mere drop upon a rose essence, the entire composition is transformed. Similarly, when applied to patchouli or sandalwood, it mellows out the arid woodiness and imparts a moist sweetness. A novel blend has been incorporated into Oud type.

Nagarmotha:	4 gm
Patchouli:	6 gm
Vetiver:	1 gm
Sandalwood:	2 gm

Bergamot: Citrus

A fragrance that leaves a lasting impression. This citrus is truly a refined and elegant creation, one that I have had the pleasure of experiencing firsthand. In my olfactory experience, it imparts a harmonious and well-rounded sense of freshness to any scent. The initial impression is not only inspiring, but it also lingers in the heart, creating a space for the weighty base notes. A gentle, wintry breeze caresses the open hilltop, accompanied by a bright, crisp sunlight that adds a hint of warmth. This ingredient is a versatile addition to many high-end fragrances, seamlessly blending with a variety of other notes.

Bergamot, when used alone in a spray, can be a complete fragrance in itself. This ingredient not only enhances freshness, but also promotes the full blossoming of the fragrance. When used skillfully, it can create a striking first impression and mask any flaws in the scent. A blend of Bergamot, Lemon, Orange, and Mandarin creates a delightful citrus aroma that lingers on the skin before transitioning to the heart notes.

Lavender: Aromatic

A warm and captivating fragrance, embodied by a beautiful and adventurous woman with smoky eyes, dressed in the attire of a cross country rider. She rides a powerful muscle bike with a relentless desire to touch the hearts of all who cross her path. A subtle hint of purple cat adds a touch of mystery to this alluring scent. This fragrance belongs to the aromatic olfactory family. The Fougere heart beats within it. The Fougere accord, consisting of Patchouli, Lavender, and Bergamot, exudes a distinctly masculine aroma. As a perfumer, I find the concept of gender in fragrances to be somewhat perplexing. To me, it's all about personal preference and the various factors that can influence our likes and dislikes. Ah, the lovely lavender - a delicate purple blossom with a lingering fragrance. This note possesses the ability to dominate, yet also has the potential to elevate or alter various scent compositions. This ingredient is widely utilized in numerous products across different regions. With a playful spirit, I experimented with substituting Patchouli and Bergamot to craft a unique Fougere.

Lavender:	5 gm
Nagarmotha:	1 gm
Lemon:	4 gm

Saffron: Floral

A fragrance that evokes a sense of independence and individuality, unbound by traditional family ties. A graceful lady adorned in orange with a violet cap, deep red shoes, and a snow-white clutch glides down the streets of Spain. I intimately collaborated with saffron. The essence of my hometown is deeply rooted in the Mughal Empire, where the mere absence of saffron fails to appease the discerning palate of the connoisseurs. Ah, the Zaffran, a beautiful name for a precious spice. Upon encountering saffron, I was enlightened that what I once believed to be the velvety strands of fruit were in fact the delicate stigmas of a flower. Through the sense of smell, some perceive it as a spice, perhaps due to its use in flavorings, while others perceive it as floral, likely due to its origin from a flower.

To my nose, this fragrance evokes a familial warmth with its musky, metallic notes and subtle hints of orris. This composition elevates the rose's sweetness, accentuates the patchouli's tobacco notes, and amplifies the oud's opulence. This element cannot be deemed a mere modifier, for it plays a crucial role in enhancing the overall performance. A precious element of opulence, radiance, and profitability, cultivated in elevated terrains. In my olfactory experience, I have found that a solitary aromatic element possesses the ability to substitute the essence of saffron when utilized at a 10% dilution.

The adulteration of natural saffron by coloring corn's hair is sometimes observed. To discern authentic saffron, place a single stigma in the center of a glass brimming with water and observe its hue. A true saffron will delicately impart a thin line of orange color that gracefully descends to the bottom of the glass, while an unnatural saffron will release its color immediately upon contact. While not commonly utilized in mainstream perfumery, it holds a significant place in the world of ittar. The essence of shamama is not fully realized without the inclusion of saffron. This exquisite attar type not only enhances the hue, but also contributes to its floral essence. Undoubtedly a luxurious element, yet its value is immeasurable.

Sandalwood: Woody

A regal and enchanting monarch, draped in robes of shimmering gold and crowned with pearls, resides within a wooden palace nestled deep within a lush forest. Sandalwood, a serene and foundational note, is a vital component in every fragrance worldwide. In the world of fragrances, numerous synthetic alternatives have emerged to mimic its distinctive essence, yet none can rival the unparalleled allure of authentic sandalwood oil. From a young age, I have been familiar with its scent, as Pita ji incorporated it into his attars as a fundamental ingredient.

For nearly a decade, I have cherished a sample that has maintained its exquisite scent, only becoming more alluring with time. The multifaceted properties of this substance are well-known, including its potential medicinal applications. In ancient times, a fragrance was crafted solely around the essence of sandalwood. Ah, sandalwood. Such a delightful aroma! Of all the varieties available, I must say that Indian sandalwood is the most pleasing to my olfactory senses, followed closely by Australian sandalwood oil.

The presence of santalol is responsible for this. In India, the art of crafting incense sticks is a cherished tradition that has been passed down through generations and has become a thriving industry. In ancient times, sandalwood dust was utilized in the creation of incense sticks. This wood exudes a refined, velvety texture with a crisp sweetness and a damp, earthy hint, complemented by a subtle waxiness. Gentle yet enduring.

Rose: Floral

An exquisite essence, revered and cherished by all cultures worldwide. The inaugural element that greets newcomers to the realm of perfumery is typically the initial ingredient. A three-dimensional red sparkle descends from the sky, dissolving into the air and leaving behind an indulgent aura that one would want to envelop themselves in and carry with them always. This fragrance embodies a floral essence with a subtle green undertone and a captivating sweetness that is truly intricate. Re-creation is simple, yet true perfection eludes even the most skilled perfumer. This essential element is the cornerstone of any complete fragrance. The floral notes tend to take center stage in women's fragrances, while a hint of these same notes can be used to add a touch of softness to men's fragrances.

It's a precious essence that requires a multitude of petals to obtain a mere few grams of its elixir. When extracting the essence of rose to create its attar, the resulting rose water has many applications, notably in the realm of beauty. Additionally, dried flowers can be utilized in the creation of incense or as decorative elements. Ah, the rose is such a ubiquitous flower, and yet, its essence varies greatly depending on its origin. I have noticed that the green notes and occasional sweetness, likely from the presence of acetates, are the key distinguishing factors. The beloved phenyl ethyl alcohol, a long-standing favorite, is a crucial component in the replication of pure rose oil's essence. This ingredient harmoniously blends with various other components, resulting in a captivating and alluring blend. As a perfumer,

I have come to appreciate that using a singular ingredient can create a complete fragrance that is beloved for its familiar scent.

Pandanus: Floral

Ah, India! The land of vibrant colors and exotic scents. Kewra, as it is known in Hindi, is a fragrance that is deeply ingrained in the culture and traditions of this beautiful country. The Pandanus flower is a rare and exquisite bloom that can only be found in the enchanting region of Orissa.

The aroma holds a surprising allure for snakes. Amidst Pandanus, one may discover an abundance beyond their initial expectations. A radiant yellow cashmere with a verdant border is showcased in a luminous glass case, drawing attention with its brilliance. A luminous hue with a delightful aroma. This fragrance possesses an unparalleled sweetness that is irreplaceable, and its bloom is undeniably potent. The top note in attars is essential for its bright freshness and ability to enhance the sweetness of the composition. Within our industry, there exists a singular aromatic element that embodies its essence – PEME- Phenyl Ethyl Methyl Ether.

This ingredient is frequently utilized in Indian breath-freshening products. The scent is utilized in laundry fragrances to capture the essence of freshly washed garments.

Sandalwood:	10 gm
Kewra:	5 gm
Rose:	3 gm

Petitgrain: Citrus

Upon encountering this ingredient, I was struck by its amusing name, which left a lasting impression. Peiti, a delicate essence reminiscent of small grains and culinary delights. The petite cuisine appears diminutive when viewed through my naive lens. Upon the initial inhalation, my olfactory senses were immediately captivated, causing a profound shift in my perception. A complex and multifaceted character, each facet playing its own unique role in the grand performance.

As a perfumer, I perceive my craft as an art form that requires mastery of various intensities, tones, and personalities, all while preserving its pristine essence. The essence of the experience is centered around a theatrical performance, where a meticulously crafted character takes center stage in a pristine white hall, illuminated by vivid green lights. The performance is reminiscent of the iconic Moulin Rouge acts of 1980s Paris. Upon further investigation of the archives, it has been revealed that petitgrain is actually derived from the leaves of the orange citrus fruit, rather than a type of grain as previously thought.

The olfactory characteristics of each component of an orange are truly remarkable to me. Petitgrain is reminiscent of fresh, crisp leaves with a citrusy aroma, while the fruit notes are sweet and juicy. Ah, petitgrain, a delightful member of the citrus family in our ingredient palette. Citrus, Fougere, and masculine fragrances rely heavily on its presence. With its green and citrus notes, this fragrance harmoniously enhances the freshness of other citrus ingredients, elevating their impact and contributing to a dynamic olfactory experience.

The best example to share the presence of Petitgrain is, the Classic 4711. The 4711 Original Eau de Cologne was launched in 1792 by Mäurer & Wirtz. A true pioneer in the world of colognes. And petitgrain, such a vital player in enhancing the freshness of the Fougere accord, while also imparting a distinct character to the fragrance's silage from start to finish. Simply divine. A harmonious blend of petitgrain, galbanum, and cedarwood, with a subtle hint of pine, evokes the essence of a pristine forest.

Petitgrain:	2 gm
Bergamot:	5 gm
Lavender:	3 gm

Nagarmotha : Woody

The renowned Cypriot oil, also known as Nagarmotha, hails from the exquisite Cypress rotundus variety of Cyperus, indigenous to the enchanting land of India. This fragrance evokes the essence of strolling through the historic streets of Old Lucknow, with a hint of nostalgia. The Mughal structure evokes a rich tapestry of memories, woven together with intricate woody notes that are both complex and alluring. The deep, earthy tones of the roots are complemented by a spicy, unique character that truly captures the essence of this remarkable structure. A luxurious and opulent ambiance is evoked by the waxy undertone, reminiscent of the lavish interiors of these edifices.

The essence of Shamama attar is crafted from the roots of Nagarmotha, a fragrant grass. One cannot craft a Shamama without it, for certain. In the realm of contemporary perfumery, oud has become a beloved ingredient in Middle Eastern markets. Nagarmotha oil is a key player in enhancing the oud/agarwood notes. Ah, the spiciness and woody notes of this ingredient truly elevate the richness and finesse of the oud.

In the world of fragrance, Ayurveda has long recognized the superficial benefits of this ingredient. It is said to aid in weight loss, strengthen hair, and offer a host of other advantages. This herb's unique properties are still being explored by researchers for its potential benefits.

My favorite accord is slightly earthy with Amber undertones.

Nagarmotha Oil:	5 gm
Iso E Super:	5 gm
Amber base:	1 gm

Cedarwood: Woody

As I inhale its essence, it evokes the image of a carpenter's workshop. As I take in the odor, I am transported to the carpenter's workshop, where he meticulously hones his tools to carve a piece of wood. The fragrance of the freshly shaved wood fills the air, revealing a dry and sharp aroma with a hint of supple softness. I perceive it as the essence of freshly cut wood. Upon encountering cedarwood, I was immediately transported to a nostalgic realm reminiscent of my school days, where the scent of freshly sharpened pencils permeated the air. As the pencil's tip is honed, the shavings delicately fall into a petite vessel, imparting a subtle essence of suede and wood. Ah, the world of perfumery! Cedarwood comes in three distinct varieties that are widely used in our craft.

Three distinct varieties of cedarwood, namely Cedarwood Himalayan, Cedarwood Virginia, and Cedarwood Texas, are widely recognized. Ah, Cedarwood China and Cedarwood Atlas, two intriguing scents that I have yet to fully explore. They possess distinct characteristics that make them stand out in their own right. Of the three commonly used, the most exquisite and costly is Cedarwood Virginia, boasting a precious note that is often utilized in velvety woody notes, whereas the Himalayan variety is utilized in incense stick perfumery. Each one possesses distinct woody accords; yet, upon comparison, one can discern the subtle nuances that set them apart and make them uniquely recognizable. To my nose, Virginia evokes the essence of Indian sandalwood, while Texas and Himalayan varieties brings to my mind the aroma of freshly cut timber planks. The inclusion of this unique element is of utmost significance in crafting a fragrance with a woody composition.

Whether it's sandalwood, oud, or a Fougere, Cedarwood embodies the authentic essence of woody notes in a fragrance.

An exquisite and velvety woody harmony that has graced my creations on numerous occasions.

Cedarwood Virginia:	5 gm
Iso E super:	4 gm
Bacdanol:	1 gm

Tree moss: Mossy

Ah, a delightful illustration of how a single aromatic element can be derived from a plethora of natural sources. Simply fascinating! Tree moss, as its name suggests, is derived from the lichens, commonly known as moss, found on pine trees in moist environments. A lush, verdant forest greets you under a serene, rainy sky, soothing your senses with its damp, earthy aroma and rejuvenating your spirit. The authentic scent of moss in its pure state is not as gentle and plush. This ingredient evokes a rich, verdant aroma with a smooth, velvety texture and subtle hints of amber. This ingredient is an essential component in the crafting of Chypre and Fougere fragrances, as it adds a necessary powdery and forest-like impression to the scent family.

Ah, in India, we have a lovely ingredient known as "Charila," or stone flower, which can serve as a delightful substitute for tree moss. Charila is a versatile ingredient that adds depth and richness to fragrances. It is often used as a strong base note in Henna and various attars and can also be found in many flavorful creations. The scarcity of Oakmoss and Tree moss has led the industry to search for suitable replacements.

Evernyl, a multifaceted replacer, is often categorized in the woody family by perfumers. However, when blended with select naturals and green notes, it can yield a highly impactful fragrance that evokes the mossy essence of natural mosses in perfumery.

Tree moss:	1 gm
Cardamom:	1 gm
Lavender:	10 gm
Bergamot:	5 gm
Patchouli:	2 gm

Benzoin: Amber

A dried resin from a tree, available in powder or block form. This fragrant substance is often referred to as "LOBAN" in the industry. A rich, earthy clay presented itself to me, its unique form beckoning me to unravel its glossy exterior and reveal its purest essence. The true essence of beauty lies beneath, as is the case with this miraculous ingredient. Its crude surface emits a faint balsamic aroma, but when crushed, it reveals a strong sweet ambery note that lingers for days.

Benzoin, a versatile ingredient in perfumery, can be employed either in its solid form or as a resinoid. The art of crafting Attars is of utmost importance, particularly in laying the foundations for the final product. This wonderful note serves as a sturdy foundation, providing a rich amber quality. In my opinion, it stands out as a top-notch natural alternative to genuine ambergris. The addition of Vanillin can truly enhance the essence of your creation.

Given that many people enjoy the way it spreads relaxing ambery tones, it is widely used in bakhoor, incense sticks, and many fumigation goods. In the art of crafting oud, sandal, amber, and other Oriental fragrances, benzoin serves as the essential cornerstone. Without it, the true essence of these scents may be lacking.

Cardamom: Spicy

This small fruit appeared to me to be a diminutive green papaya. Amusingly, it bears no resemblance to its botanical lineage. The opulence of this wonder spice used ubiquitously in Indian cuisine is truly noble in essence. As you unravel the thread of this emerald purse, a bouquet of fresh greens and warm luxury emanates from within, accented by the glimmering black diamonds nestled inside.

The sparkling freshness of each diamond is robust. Ah, the exquisite aroma of cardamom! Truly, one of nature's finest treasures, encapsulated in such a small and delicate package. The fragrance emanating from the seed and shell is a distinct blend of sweet, fresh, metallic, green, and aromatic notes, with occasional hints of herbal undertones. Cardamom is a highly significant ingredient in the F&F industry.

The Indian desserts are enriched by its flavor, while in fragrances it adds a touch of freshness to classic Orientals and chypre. In attars, it plays the dual roles of both flavor and fragrance. A blend of saffron, cloves, nutmeg, and mace are commonly incorporated to infuse an attar with a lively, spicy, and invigorating essence. In India, the market for mouth fresheners is vast and diverse. One can find silver-coated cardamoms infused with a variety of sweet condiments, often sold at a premium price. Ah, cardamom! Such a delightful ingredient, with its high chemical composition of limonene, eucalyptol, and linalool. It truly captures the essence of freshness with its unique blend of aromatic notes. And let's not forget the luxurious warmth that envelops each and every seed and fruit, creating a harmonious balance of scents. Simply divine! Seldom employed in exquisite perfumery, it's a fragrant element frequently found in masala chai and also utilized in Hindu devotions.

Cardamom:	0.5 gm
Safranal:	0.5 gm
Rose:	10 gm
Sandal:	4 gm

Black pepper: Spicy

An ingredient frequently encountered in the Indian kitchen. This berry is a member of the Piperecia family, offering a vast array of fragrances. Ah, the subtle yet powerful black pepper. It has the ability to add a touch of spice to any formulation with just the slightest amount. A stunning, youthful bohemian is presented, adorned in a sleek black silk dress, captured in a monochromatic vector frame. The lingering image evokes a fresh sensation of black hues that lasts throughout the day in one's memory. Infrequently, deep hues are not typically associated with freshness.

However, black pepper is a noteworthy element utilized in perfumery to invigorate the senses with a burst of freshness, enhancing the citrus notes and adding a twist to the woodsy aroma. This essence is highly volatile and exclusively present in the impression's notes. A heavier application could result in sharpness, as the oil possesses a highly concentrated profile.

The subtle yet enigmatic freshness of this note adds a captivating finishing touch to any fragrance, provided it is paired with the right notes. The fragrance begins with a refreshing aquatic note that quickly dissipates, giving way to a warm, woody, and spicy aroma that lingers on the skin. Throughout the ages, perfumers have cherished the versatile and timeless aroma of pepper, incorporating it into both traditional and contemporary fragrances. This ingredient finds its place in the creation of both scents and tastes. The intriguing woody undertones of black pepper caught my attention. While some may perceive it as herbal or aromatic, I find it to be velvety and hot.

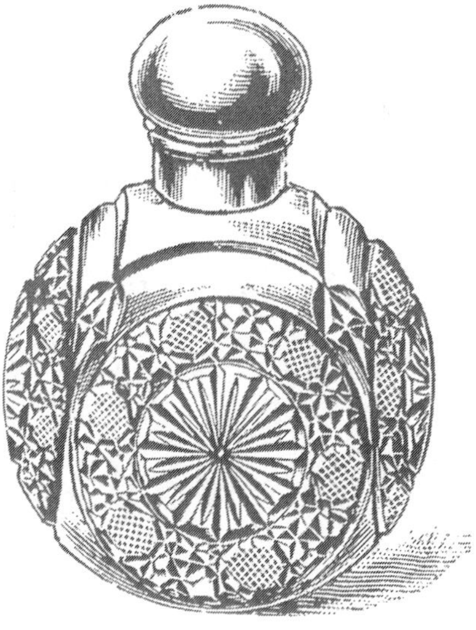

Adventure with Synthetic Ingredients

How to approach and learn Synthetic aroma Ingredients?

Embarking on a journey through the realm of synthetic compounds utilized in perfumery can be a fascinating and stimulating expedition for the imaginative mind. The art of perfumery has been elevated to new heights with the advent of synthetic components, providing perfumers with an unparalleled range of possibilities to craft unique and intricate fragrances. With these substances, perfumers can explore a remarkable range of scents that would be challenging to achieve solely with natural components.

As you explore the realm of synthetic perfumery ingredients, you'll uncover the delicate intricacies of each component and their interplay. As you delve deeper into the realm of synthetic perfumery ingredients, this realization will gradually unfold. Through the art of perfumery, one can master the art of combining various components to create fragrances that evoke emotions, memories, and transport individuals to different times and places. It is a way to enhance the beauty and complexity of the natural world around us.

To truly comprehend the elements of synthetic fragrances, one must exercise a certain level of creativity. Crafting unique scents requires perfumers to possess a keen imagination and a daring spirit to explore and test various elements. A perfumer must possess the skill of harmoniously balancing the various components of a fragrance, meticulously layering each element to create a product that is both pleasing to the senses and visually stunning.

Crafting fragrances involves mastering the delicate balance between artistry and scientific understanding of synthetic compounds. To create a truly unique and exquisite product, one must possess a thorough understanding of the chemical properties of each element, and a creative flair for blending and layering those elements.

Ambroxan: Amber

The presence of ambergris in its natural habitat is widely known, as documented in various literary works and historical records. The olfactory experience proved to be quite challenging to envision, considering its origin as a byproduct of the digestive system of a whale. Discovering such a rarity is truly exceptional in modern times.

After years of research and experimentation, we are pleased to acknowledge the efforts of our colleagues in the industry and scientific community for creating a viable substitute. Ah, ambroxan, my dear "White Gold". It may not dazzle with a sparkle, but it radiates with a brilliance akin to that of a 6000-K white LED bulb. Ambroxan was developed in the 1950s as a replacement for ambergris, largely used in oriental fragrances

The scent opens with a delicate flurry of snowflakes, descending from the vast expanse of the evening sky. As it settles into the arid terrain of the Arabian countryside, its opulent weight spreads for miles, enveloping all who encounter it. The subtle amber profile of this fragrance is elevated by its high threshold, ensuring its presence is prominent even when diluted. Rare is the contemporary fragrance that could thrive without the inclusion of this opulent substance.

In Gandhavadha, reference dated 1961, it mentions that between the years 700 and 1000 A.D. and later, the terms Ambara, Ambar, Ambrum, Ambergris, Ambergreece, and Anbar were used to refer to Ambergris. In India, the term "Matsyika" (meaning "product from fish") was also used to refer to it around the year 1676 A.D.

Tavernier's A.D. 1676 travel through India resulted in the recording of some insightful comments about ambergris, which can be found in some of his books. It appears that we do not know how it is generated, but it can be found occasionally in the waters off the beaches of England and Europe. People from Mozambique would make the trip every three years to bring it to Goa in India.

As a perfumer, I utilize ambergris as a foundational note and artfully combine it with other exquisite natural elements such as patchouli, vetiver, or nagarmotha to craft a captivating fragrance. The oud essence is a vital element in the composition of a perfume. My composition features a blend of nagarmotha, ambroxan, cedramber, and patchouli in carefully measured proportions. An excessive amount of ambroxan can be counterproductive, as it may hinder the fragrance's diffusion for several days.

The objective behind incorporating fragrances in various products, such as shampoos, detergents, soaps, and creams, is to ensure that they do not dissipate quickly and remain on the surface even after application. The longevity of the fragrance is enhanced, while the overall character of the scent is given definition, particularly in the case of masculine fragrances.

This ingredient enhances the sandalwood aroma and provides a strong base for floral scents, especially rose, while also adding a delicate and captivating touch to fruity notes.

Ethylene Brassylate: Musk

This fragrance is commonly known as Musk T. The essence of this musk molecule is a rare discovery that I have encountered in my journey. The olfactory perception of musk can be elusive for some due to biological factors. Even for those who possess the ability to detect musk, it takes a certain level of expertise and experience to discern the distinct elements that comprise this fragrance. Through the creation of musk, it is widely known that this fragrance originates from a majestic animal of the deer family, found in the lofty heights of the Himalayan mountains. A worldwide limitation has been imposed on the acquisition of animal-derived components. In response to the historical ban and to safeguard the natural resource, chemical companies developed synthetic molecules that closely mimic the suede, velvety, and animalistic notes of natural musk. Musk is an essential element in every fragrance. Not only does it guarantee the longevity of a scent but also makes a substantial contribution to its composition and provides distinct delineations.

The Musk T fragrance, discovered in the 1960s, I assume, evokes the image of a graceful, soulful deer traversing the snowy Arctic landscape at dawn, illuminated by the sparkling light of the rising sun. The scent captures the essence of this serene and majestic moment. The serene ambiance evokes a sense of wonder as the glistening snow blends seamlessly with the essence of the deer. Upon experiencing Musk T, I detect a smooth and velvety texture, with a pristine and pure essence. Subtle nuances of animalistic undertones linger in the background. Over time, the strip reveals a captivating velvety essence that becomes increasingly prominent.

Musk T:	10 gm
Iso E super:	12 gm
DHM:	8 gm

Triplal: Green

I was captivated by an element that embodies the essence of a grass, transforming its appearance over time and presenting a new and vibrant image for your senses to capture in any season and diverse locations across the globe. The verdant essence of grass is a sensory journey through the natural world, elevating your senses to a heightened state of awareness. Triplal evokes the vibrant essence of lush green grass in the summertime of Johannesburg.

The aroma of triplal, or tricylal, evokes the essence of newly mown grass in a verdant garden. This fragrance evokes the essence of a freshly cut garden, lending a refreshing and natural quality to any blend. For optimal olfactory experience, it is recommended to appreciate the aroma in a 10% dilution. At times, its crisp essence, when blended with succulent apple notes, evokes the sensation of a freshly picked green apple, while when fused with lemon notes, it exudes the essence of freshly squeezed lemon. A delicate blend of zesty lime and fragrant floral notes, with a prominent essence of rose that enhances the bouquet of budding flowers.

In the art of perfumery, the essence of green notes is of utmost importance. However, achieving the perfect balance requires a delicate touch, as they must be used sparingly. The reason being that, at elevated concentrations, green notes possess the potential to dominate the top notes and present themselves as abrasive. The absence of certain natural elements, such as florals, fruits, and aromatic fragrances, would render the creation incomplete.

Classic Accord	
Triplal 10% dilution :	0.5 gm
Evernyl :	0.5 gm
Patchouli :	1 gm
Petitgrain :	2.5 gm
Linalool :	3 gm
Lemon oil :	3 gm

Hedione: Floral

Ah, Hedione, the exquisite synthetic compound also referred to as methyl dihydrojasmonate, is a beloved ingredient in the world of perfumery. Its delicate essence imbues fragrances with a refreshing, floral, and subtly fruity aroma.

It's a radiant burst of sunshine on a warm summer day, evoking joy and positivity in every scent. A delicate floral bouquet with hints of jasmine, orange blossom, and ylang-ylang is detected in the scent. The addition of this subtle yet essential element brings a complexity to numerous fragrances, infusing them with a sense of vitality and vibrancy.

Hedione's crisp and ethereal essence evokes the sensation of inhaling a pure and refreshing breeze. It is exceptionally useful in creating fragrances that exude a peaceful and tranquil ambiance. This ingredient imbues the fragrance with a hint of allure and closeness.

This multifaceted and popular element in the world of perfumery is adored for its delightful blend of fresh, floral, and fruity aromas that can imbue any scent with a sense of wonder and allure.

Discovered In 1950s, the exquisite fragrances of Ck One, Aqua Di Gio, and Jadore have skillfully incorporated a lavish amount of this ingredient to accentuate its finest qualities, resulting in a remarkable and alluring trail.

Vanillin: Sweet

This ingredient possesses a multitude of facets that unfold as it is utilized. This ingredient offers a diverse range of expressions, depending on its concentration within a composition. To prevent discoloration in a product, it is crucial to comprehend its chemistry. However, in certain instances, the use of the following notes cannot be avoided.

The fragrance exudes a cozy and inviting aura, with the addition of vanillin providing a comforting warmth that evokes a sense of comfort and snugness.

A velvety and luscious aroma, it possesses a rich and creamy sweetness that can infuse fragrances with depth and intricacy.

The alluring and amorous essence of vanillin can elicit sensations of sensuality and romance, rendering it a favored option in seductive scents.

The comforting and familiar aroma of vanilla is a popular choice in nostalgic fragrances, as it evokes a sense of nostalgia and comfort. Vanillin is a commonly used ingredient in such fragrances.

Vanillin is a perfect ingredient to craft fragrances that evoke a sense of comfort and coziness, reminiscent of a warm embrace on a chilly day.

Indulgent and delectable: The luscious and velvety essence of vanillin can conjure up visions of scrumptious confections and delicacies, rendering it a favored option in gourmand perfumes.

The gentle and velvety notes of vanillin can be skillfully blended to produce a tender and powdery aroma, evoking a sense of delicacy and femininity in fragrances.

Vanillin, a beloved aroma chemical in perfumery, exudes a sweet, creamy, and warm vanilla-like fragrance. This note is frequently utilized as a foundation in perfumes and can be detected in culinary and beauty items.

Linalool: Citrus

Ah, Linalool! A delightful top note that adds a bright and sparkling quality to fragrances. This fragrance evokes a fresh and zesty essence, akin to the bright notes of bergamot or lemon, yet exuding a subtle and refined quality.

This note is present in numerous floral essential oils, including lavender, rose, and neroli, and imparts a delightful, floral character to fragrances. It has a floral essence, reminiscent of blooming blossoms or the sweet aroma of just-cut flowers.

Often characterized as having a verdant and herbaceous aroma, reminiscent of freshly crushed foliage.

The essence of linalool exudes a pristine and refreshing aura, evoking a feeling of immaculacy and clarity in perfumes. This ingredient is frequently utilized in soap and detergent formulations due to its invigorating and refreshing qualities.

The fragrance of linalool is appreciated for its refreshing, flowery, and subtly piquant aroma.

Coumarin: Hay

A delightful ingredient that has graced the world of perfumery for many years with its alluring fragrance. The scent of coumarin possesses a delightful essence reminiscent of sweet hay, complemented by delicate hints of vanilla and almond.

Its comforting and inviting qualities make it a beloved option for crafting cozy and inviting perfumes.

Coumarin is an incredibly versatile and expressive ingredient, as I perceive it.

Coumarin, with its long-lasting and potent aroma, is a remarkable base note that is frequently incorporated into various fragrances. This ingredient possesses the ability to infuse a perfume with warmth, depth, and complexity. Its sweet and comforting aroma renders it a perfect fit for fragrances designed for the autumn and winter seasons. When crafting a Fougere, one must pay close attention to its usage, as it contributes to the overall warmth of the composition.

The scent reminiscent of hay has the ability to enhance the essence of floral fragrances. With a delicate touch, it has the ability to infuse a subtle sweetness into floral notes, resulting in a beautifully balanced fragrance.

Coumarin's warm and inviting nature renders it a perfect component for crafting exquisite oriental scents. The addition of this ingredient can enhance the complexity and allure of spicy notes such as cinnamon and cardamom, resulting in a rich and mysterious fragrance.

With a keen understanding of its application, one can craft delightful fragrances reminiscent of caramel, chocolate, and coffee.

Iso E Super: Woody

Iso E Super, a potent and multifaceted aroma compound that has graced the world of perfumery for countless years, boasts of a sophisticated and contemporary aroma with notes of wood, musk, and earth.

The velvety texture and smooth finish of Iso E Super evoke an atmosphere of understated elegance and refinement. The comforting and alluring fragrance is achieved by perfectly balancing the warm and woody notes of Iso E Super with a hint of sweetness.

Iso E Super is a remarkable ingredient that brings depth, complexity, and a touch of elegance to any fragrance.

It is akin to a clandestine tool in the arsenal of perfumers, imbuing each scent it graces with a hint of enchantment.

In the art of perfumery, the addition of this ingredient works wonders in enhancing the body of the velvety, warm, and sweet natural Indian oud type, resulting in an alluring fragrance.

Peach Pure: Fruity

This is a delightful ingredient, often referred to as Aldehyde C14.

A crisp and refreshing fragrance reminiscent of freshly washed cotton, leaving a subtle and clean aroma on the skin. It infuses a contemporary touch into traditional floral blends, imparting a revitalizing and effervescent sensation that elevates the entire scent. This ingredient has the potential to infuse fragrances with a cool and metallic essence, lending a futuristic and sophisticated aura to the final blend. A delicate aroma with a subtle waxiness and a touch of verdancy.

The Aldehyde C14 exhibits a fruity essence akin to the aroma of luscious fruits such as peaches, pears, or apples. It possesses the ability to infuse a succulent and fruity sweetness into a fragrance, or harmoniously enhance other fruity notes within a more intricate composition.

One of the best examples to learn from the history of fragrances is Mitsouko, a legendary fragrance made by Guerlain, the prestigious French perfume manufacturer. It was first introduced in 1919 and has since become a perfumery timeless classic.

Mitsouko's allure is enhanced by Aldehyde C-14, a rich and delicious peach tone that dominates the start of Mitsouko. This fruity accord introduces the aroma in a sweet and succulent manner, lending it a delicate and inviting character, followed by its Chypre signature with oakmoss, which gives the perfume a rich and earthy tone, creating the impression of wandering through a forest. The oakmoss note adds duration and richness to the smell.

Aldehyde C 12 MNA: Aldehydic Floral

This ingredient imparts a lively and bubbly character to every scent. This note is frequently blended with other aldehydes to produce a luminous and ethereal impression, evocative of the effervescence found in champagne or sparkling wine. With the incorporation of aldehyde C12 MNA, the fragrance's other notes can be elevated and intensified, resulting in a more enduring and noticeable scent.

This note possesses a subtle, velvety texture that can be artfully blended to produce opulent and indulgent olfactory experiences. This ingredient has the ability to enhance the luxurious texture of floral or woody scents, or to impart a delicate, powdery touch to a perfume.

An invigorating scent is crafted by blending it with crisp, clean notes like citrus, green, and aquatic notes to produce a revitalizing aroma. This fragrance can be beautifully complemented by floral accords such as jasmine, rose, or lily-of-the-valley, imparting a delicate and fresh dewiness to the scent.

Aldehyde C12 MNA, the beautiful lauryl aldehyde or dodecanal, a potent aldehyde that finds its place in the world of perfumery. This fragrance boasts a refreshing and pure aroma, with delicate hints of floral and fruity notes. It is a popular choice as a top note in many perfumes.

Please smell it only in dilutions of 10% or lower.

The Exploration of Harmony, "Accords"

What are fragrance accords?

In the realm of perfumery, much like any other field of expertise, there exist distinguished famous people whose footsteps are followed by all. One such revered figure is Sir Jean Carles, the artisan whose techniques and fragrant compositions continue to inspire students at perfumery academies. The author's articles on the art of perfumery, dating back to 1961, have been distilled to a level of simplicity that allows for self-guided learning, as I have experienced firsthand.

The fledgling perfumer, in the early stages of their journey, is akin to a vessel adrift without a guiding compass. When one is not properly guided or left to their own accord, their creative ideas may become disorganized, and their energy may be expended in unproductive ways.

After understanding ingredients for at least the first half of their study, you must now learn to make accords. An accord is a frequently used term in the world of perfumery as you delve deeper into the craft. As a perfumer, your task is to blend two ingredients, whether from the same or different fragrance families, to create a harmonious and distinctive scent that strikes the perfect balance of profiles. The esteemed Sir Jean Carles has bestowed upon us a newfound ease. In the art of perfumery, we adhere to a unique method for crafting and mastering accords. Our approach involves blending ingredients in precise ratios, ranging from 1:9 to 9:1. This technique not only cultivates a sense of balance but also yields the most exquisite results. It seems that my forefathers did not chance upon this technique. Instead, they relied on their olfactory senses to detect the nuances of each ingredient and envisioned the perfect ratios to achieve a harmonious blend. The optimal blend was achieved by harmoniously combining them in a ratio of 50:50 or 75:25, resulting in a delightful olfactory experience. The foundation of any olfactory creation lies in the accord. To achieve a lasting signature, one must possess a deep understanding of and skill in crafting accords. Ah, the memory of my first accord in my father's lab lingers on. Patchouli 6 and Geranium 4 were the stars of the show, and I simply had to extend their beauty. With the addition of sandalwood, the result was nothing short of lovely.

Patchouli	3 g
Geranium	2 g
Sandalwood	2 g
Vetiver	1 g

I was able to craft a luxurious Oriental base note, featuring sweet, woody, floral, and ambery accord. This exquisite blend is perfect for creating opulent attars.

In essence, just as a musical composition must have a harmonious flow, so too must a fragrance. If one has a passion for music, the same can be said for the art of perfumery. The harmonious accord, similar to the balance of cords, is the ultimate goal in achieving a seamless flow.

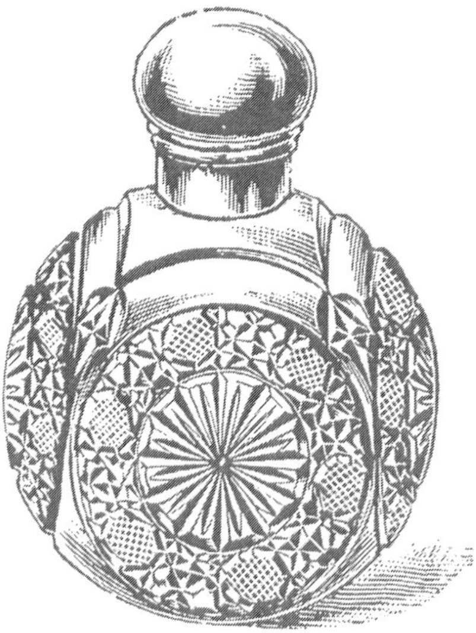

Fragrance Insights and Perspectives

How to evaluate fragrances ?

The art of perfumery relies heavily on the evaluation of fragrances as a foundation for innovative creations. A discerning individual who can analyze and provide critiques to fragrances has the potential to excel as an evaluator. To attain this esteemed title, one must possess not only a keen sense of smell, but also exceptional project management skills, a vivid imagination, boundless creativity, and a true artistic flair. Additionally, a deep understanding of the consumer is essential. Having spent years as an evaluator, I have gained a wider perspective on the art of perfumery.

In the year 2013, I embarked on a journey to cultivate my passion and delve deeper into the enchanting realm of fragrances. Upon accepting my role as a fragrance evaluator, my intention was to gain a deeper understanding of the industry through various perspectives and the lens of the consumer.

The art of perfumery involves meticulously evaluating and discerning the essence of a fragrance, assessing its strength, richness, and endurance. This step is absolutely essential in the art of perfumery, as it guarantees that the scent attains the desired level of excellence. The art of fragrance creation encompasses a series of meticulous stages, from crafting the perfect scent to ensuring its longevity and conducting a sensory assessment. In this article, we shall delve into the intricate process of evaluating fragrances step by step.

The initial phase of olfactory assessment entails the creation of a scent. Perfumers collaborate with perfume manufacturers to craft a scent concept that fulfils the desired criteria. The art of perfumery involves crafting a unique scent composition by harmoniously blending essential oils, aroma chemicals, and various other ingredients. The composition is subsequently evaluated for steadfastness to guarantee the aroma's constancy throughout its lifespan. Stability testing is a crucial aspect of fragrance creation, as it guarantees that the scent retains its intended aroma, hue, and consistency.

In the art of perfumery, the second phase of fragrance evaluation involves conducting stability testing. The stability testing process involves evaluating the fragrance formula's capacity to sustain its intended aroma, hue, and consistency throughout its lifespan. As a fragrance expert, diverse evaluation techniques are employed to assess the steadfastness of a scent. Our olfactory assessment techniques encompass evaluations of temperature, light, and pH sensitivities.

The olfactory assessment comprises subjecting the scent to varying temperatures to discern its response. This evaluation aids in assessing the olfactory and textural variations of the fragrance under varying temperatures. The olfactory assessment comprises subjecting the perfume to diverse luminous environments to ascertain any chromatic or aromatic alterations upon light exposure. The pH testing process entails scrutinizing the acidity or alkalinity of the scent to ascertain its impact on the fragrance's steadfastness.

The ultimate phase of olfactory assessment involves sensory analysis. The art of perfumery involves a meticulous examination of a fragrance's olfactory profile, strength, and staying power through sensory analysis. Trained olfactory experts are employed by perfumers to assess the sensory characteristics of fragrances. A group of skilled individuals, with a refined sense of smell, form the sensory panel. They meticulously assess the aroma's notes, strength, and staying power.

The expert panel assesses the fragrance through olfactory analysis, carefully evaluating its intensity, quality, and longevity. The intensity of the aroma is the potency of the perfume, whereas the quality of the scent pertains to the fragrance's overall olfactory profile. The olfactory persistence pertains to the duration of the scent's endurance post-application. To create a captivating fragrance, one must first comprehend the fundamental benchmarks of the scent they aim to craft. Only after delving deeply into this can you truly fine-tune your choices and attain mastery. This olfactory assessment greatly aids perfumers in refining their craft to attain consumer appeal. Creating a fragrance is no easy feat, as it requires months of meticulous evaluation to hone this craft.

The olfactory assessment of fragrances Is of utmost importance in guaranteeing that scents satisfy the desires of the consumer and that the items that bear them are prosperous in the market.

A key phase of assessment involves identifying the intended demographic. Understanding the preferences and expectations of our valued customers is essential in crafting the perfect scent profile for our product. A youthful fragrance may feature fruity or floral notes, whereas a mature fragrance may showcase a musky or woody aroma. To craft a captivating scent, one must comprehend the intended audience's preferences. The craft involves utilizing a variety of techniques but also consumer testing.

The olfactory assessment entails inhaling the aroma and discerning its distinct elements, including the head, heart, and base accords. The olfactory experts employ their sense of scent to discern the potency, longevity, and overall excellence of the aroma.

The olfactory evaluation process entails gathering input from prospective clients regarding the aroma. Gathering valuable insights through meticulous surveys, discerning focus groups, and other refined market research techniques. The evaluation of the fragrance by the consumers is crucial to ascertain if it meets their expectations and to detect any potential areas of enhancement. By discerning the fragrance's unique characteristics, one may uncover untapped niche markets that it could captivate.

Perfumers utilize a variety of standards to evaluate fragrances. These factors encompass potency, longevity, and overall character. The intensity of a fragrance is a measure of its potency, while its duration is a reflection of its staying power.

The essence's overall quality encompasses its allure, harmony, and distinctiveness.

Apart from these standards, fragrance assessors also take into account elements like prevailing market trends, rival products, and regulatory obligations. The olfactory character of a product can be influenced by prevailing market trends, while the offerings of competitors can offer valuable insights into the desires of discerning consumers.

It is recommended that one possess a degree in chemistry or a related scientific field in order to pursue a career as a fragrance evaluator. It is because you must work with fine fragrances and consumer products.

The intricate chemistry of these end products allows for a meticulous evaluation of the scent's potential.

In the world of perfumery, fragrance development is categorized into two main segments: consumer products and fine fragrances. Consumer products encompass a wide range of items, such as soaps, detergents, creams, shampoos, makeup, and more. To simplify, we call them personal care, which focuses on fragrances for products used on your body and fabric care which focuses on laundry. The Fine Fragrances segment, also known as parfum or spray perfumes, is another significant aspect of our craft. In the realm of fine fragrances, we classify them according to their perfume concentration and refer to them as EDTs or EDPs.

Throughout my years, I have been fortunate enough to have been exposed to a wide range of categories, but I have developed a unique expertise in personal care, which I find to be quite delightful.

In the realm of personal care fragrance evaluation, one must first grasp the essence of the product in question. To truly appreciate the artistry of each format, one must possess a deep understanding of its fundamentals before embarking on the journey of infusing it with the meticulously crafted fragrance. Before deciding on the design and evaluation of a fragrance for a specific format, it is crucial to delve into the chemistry, formulation, and manufacturing process of the product. Understanding these fundamental aspects lays the foundation for creating a captivating olfactory experience. Personal care is an expansive realm, encompassing a vast array of exquisite offerings. Within this realm, one may discover an assortment of body creams, lotions, bathing soaps, and handwashes rich in texture and fragrance. Additionally, this sector has an assortment of captivating anti-perspirants, each meticulously crafted to enhance one's personal grooming experience. In essence, any product that graces the body and caresses the skin can be elegantly categorized under the realm of personal care. As a fragrance evaluator, it is essential to possess a comprehensive understanding of skin biology, with even a basic knowledge being sufficient to begin the evaluation process.

Fragrance evaluation plays a vital role in the development of personal care products, as it exerts a profound impact on consumer perception and the overall acceptability of the product. In the captivating realm of fragrance evaluation, we embark on a journey to discern the essence's captivating character, its alluring intensity, and its enduring longevity.

Our discerning senses delicately explore the harmonious compatibility between this olfactory masterpiece and the exquisite base formulation of the product. A masterfully crafted fragrance evaluation elevates the holistic product encounter and encapsulates the essence of the brand.

The olfactory exploration commences with the careful curation of prospective fragrances, meticulously chosen to align with the desired essence and allure of the product, captivating the discerning senses of the intended clientele. In the captivating world of fragrance houses, a splendid array of options is meticulously crafted, each one a masterpiece waiting to be discovered. With utmost care and discernment, product developers embark on a journey to select a select few candidates, destined to undergo a profound evaluation, where their essence shall be revealed and their true allure displayed. The olfactory examination commences with a series of delicate sniff tests, allowing the fragrance to gracefully dance upon the senses. Subsequently, a gentle application upon the skin unveils the true essence of the composition. This exquisite stage gracefully guides the discerning individual towards a refined selection, preparing the way for more elaborate assessments.

Consumer panels are of utmost importance in the subsequent stages of fragrance evaluation. A team of highly skilled panelists, consisting of esteemed fragrance connoisseurs and individuals who embody the essence of our desired audience, meticulously carry out sensory assessments. The exquisite art of fragrance evaluation unveils a world of sensory delights, where quantitative measures like descriptive analysis and sensory profiling gracefully dance together. These measures gracefully unravel the intricate weaving of attributes, revealing the delicate nuances of sweetness, the invigorating essence of freshness, and the captivating allure of overall appeal. The exquisite nature of qualitative feedback allows for the discernment of any unfavorable characteristics or the possibility of sensitivities.

The enchanting fragrance undergoes compatibility testing, gracefully blending into the product matrix at different concentrations. Stability tests are crucial in ensuring that the fragrance maintains its harmonious composition throughout the product's shelf life. Compatibility plays a pivotal role in intricate formulations such as creams and lotions, where the potential interactions with various ingredients have the ability to subtly transform the fragrance profile.

The art of concentration optimization takes centerstage as we delve into the realm of exploring the nuances of fragrance load variations. This delicate dance allows us to uncover the perfect balance, unveiling the ideal strength that will effortlessly captivate and evoke the desired effect. In this olfactory journey, utmost precision is paramount to delicately harmonize an alluring aroma with the delicate nuances of potential skin sensitivities. The fragrance's performance is meticulously evaluated under various usage conditions, including the challenging hot and humid environments.

The longevity testing method assesses the fragrance's ability to linger gracefully on the skin.

Consumer testing in real-world scenarios is an invaluable

opportunity to gain profound insights into the holistic product experience. Through the utilization of focus groups or larger-scale trials, the fragrance is meticulously assessed in real-life scenarios, allowing for a comprehensive evaluation of its impact. This process enables the refinement of the formulation, ensuring its optimal performance and satisfaction.

When it comes to toilet soaps and creams, it is crucial to delve into the field of fragrance evaluation. This intricate process commences by meticulously examining the harmonious interplay between the selected fragrance and the product base. The fragrance's ability to maintain its stability and authenticity within the product matrix is of utmost importance. The exquisite balance of the fragrance dosage not only enhances the product's stability but also elevates the overall olfactory journey, promising to fulfil the lofty expectations of discerning consumers.

Apart from olfactory assessment, perfumers also employ instrumental analysis to assess the chemical makeup of a fragrance. The art of perfumery entails the utilization of analytical equipment, such as gas chromatography-mass spectrometry (GC-MS) or headspace analysis, to scrutinize the chemical composition of the fragrance. This olfactory examination yields precious insights into the scent's molecular composition and aids in detecting any flaws or pollutants that could compromise its excellence.

Crafting Memories

How to capture moments for your creation?

The symphony is a harmonious blend of diverse instruments, each with its own unique tuning. The composer meticulously adjusts the cords of each instrument to create a masterpiece of sound. Thus, it lies within the realm of the art of painting. With a discerning eye, the master artist selects from a myriad of hues to craft a masterpiece that captures the very essence of their creative vision. The culmination of any artistry lies in capturing and ultimately presenting it to the world.

Nowadays, you can quickly capture any picture, moment, object, or personality with the camera on your phone, whereas, a few decades ago, this was only possible with digital cameras or by making sketches on canvas. It is very well observed, photography and painting still have a special ability to catch fine details that are more expressive and effectively convey emotion.

Visually recording memories is a necessary first step in perfumery. It takes a thoughtful method to translate the captured image into a bottle; one must further characterize each part of the scene, time, object, or personality by translating them into olfactory families, and then transport the same with ingredients to create a perfume.

With the help of the excellent instrument of mind mapping, one can approach this practice methodically. But eventually, in order to create a perfume that accurately captures the images, one must understand which part to emphasize most and balance the others.

It may not always provide one's recollection the full picture when a situation is expressed through a scent, but the art of perfumery undoubtedly conveys the sensations, emotions, and sense of scents that were present in that scene, which is, in certain capacities, highly artistic.

As I travelled to many locations, I tried to record special events with my passable memory. I maintained the realization of these experiences and turned them into perfumes.

The Indian Wedding

I had already determined that I would adhere to my parents' cultural preferences for my marriage. I preferred a formal arranged wedding, and it was evident that I would accept the first person I met in person. Rejecting someone based on my own idealistic beliefs seemed imprudent, as encountering the next person would only add to my confusion. The olfactory experience of traditional Punjabi weddings has always captivated my senses.

Haldi – Everything is yellow.

A delicate rub of homemade turmeric scrub is applied, imbuing a yellow hue. This is a ceremony, but in truth, it will imbue you with a radiant and alluring aura for your wedding evening. Upon first opening, the beauty paste reveals a fresh and spicy aroma with woody and dry undertones. A sharp, slightly aldehydic note emerges, which then evolves into a wheatish and musky scent reminiscent of chickpea flour. As the fragrance develops, it transforms into a milky aroma, reminiscent of thick curd, which effectively balances out the sharpness. Finally, the scent takes on a more yellow hue when mixed with a spoonful of yellow mustard oil. The space is adorned with the vibrant essence of marigold flowers, delicately balanced with the soft elegance of white satin to enhance its radiance. The air is filled with the sweet melodies of Punjabi folk songs. The rhythmic ceremony is a symphony of scents.

Mehndi – The Floral tattoo

The essence of this ritual is familiar to various communities across India. Weaving scents is not only a task, but also a sacred ritual in many religious festivities. Mehndi is a delicate floral scent that captures the sweetness of sugarcane and the freshness of jasmine. Its floral notes are captivating and blooming, yet not overpowering. Ah, the delicate leaf of the Mehndi plant! It is this humble leaf that lends its precious essence to the sacred paste, not the flower. This paste exudes a rich, dark amber aroma with notes of tea and coffee, complemented by warm clove spices and the delicate, green scent of Mehndi flowers. The exquisite hue of the paste is attributed to the pivotal contribution of the Catechu tannins.

The fragrance is delicately applied with ornate cones onto the palms and wrists, and as it settles, its aroma becomes more potent. The Osmanthus fruitiness is a scent that I have long desired to incorporate. The fragrance is not the primary focus, but rather the design. When a ceremony filled with emotions, where the bride prepares to depart from her childhood abode, comes to a close, a nostalgic journey down memory lane ensues.

Wedding Day – La Vie N Rose

The occasion takes place in a grand venue adorned with vibrant hues of pink, white, gold, silver, and, occasionally, a hint of blue. The luminosity is perfectly balanced. Upon entering, a treasure trove of floral scents envelops you. The jubilant atmosphere exudes a sense of joy and elation, evoking a feeling of being immersed in the festivities. The alluring scent of the red rose, with its sweet and petal-like aroma, harmonizes perfectly with the rich and intoxicating fragrance of jasmine, enhanced by the refreshing and citrusy notes of marigold. At the start, a gentle melody of clarinet or flute can be heard in the distance. Suddenly, as the groom makes his entrance, the atmosphere explodes with the vibrant beat of the dhol and dhamaaka. The energy in the room is obvious. As the rituals commence, a hush falls over the entire space.

My Elixir –	
Red Rose:	10 g
Jasmine:	1 g
Marigold:	1 g
Sandal Base:	3 g

Osmanthus – Pudong memories

The crisp air of Shanghai's first winter greeted me as I prepared for my morning run. The memory of that moment lingers on my mind, as I emerged from my abode. As a perfumer, I couldn't help but notice the powerful aroma emanating from someone nearby. It seemed to fill the entire staircase, reminiscent of the sweet and fruity scent of ripe peaches. As I strolled down the streets, I couldn't help but notice the lingering fruity notes that enveloped me, following me for kilometers and filling my senses. I paused to inhale the delicate aroma of the nearby yellow blossoms. Oh! The delicate essence of Osmanthus. The scent was a novel experience for my olfactory senses. The natural world is truly exquisite. A fruity essence, with a complexity that is truly captivating. To my nose, it evokes the alluring aroma of peach skin, with hints of sweet apricot and the verdant essence of henna. The scent permeated the entire street, evoking a beautiful sensation. Ah, the exquisite Osmanthus. How delightful it would be to create an attar of this precious flower. Discovering the true essence of osmanthus has been a valuable lesson for me. While it has often been incorporated into fragrances, I have come to appreciate it as a standalone accord. The essence lies in ionone and lactones, and it smells really good. It has a sweet and floral scent with a hint of musk.

Alpha Ionone:	7 g
Beta Ionone :	10 g
C – 14:	10 g
DMBCB:	3 g

Camps Bay Beach – First family vacation, South Africa.

It was a cherished memory of a familial escapade during our sojourn in South Africa, more specifically, Cape town, a dreamy destination that has finally invited me to indulge in its heavenly essence. On a Sunday morning, the beginning of summer, I found myself at Camp's Bay, situated in the Atlantic Ocean. The chilly breeze was beyond my olfactory expectations. The gentle, powdery sand encircling the bay of crystal blue waters caresses your senses with a crisp, refreshing oceanic aroma. As you immerse yourself in this breathtaking vista, a sense of tranquility washes over you. The vibrant melody of swaying palm trees harmonizes with the alluring musk of oceanic creatures, entwining with the refreshing scent of seaweed and a hint of briny sparkle that lingers in my presence. The pure white clouds embracing the majestic Table Mountain, just beyond the shore, contribute to the fragrance of the moment. A cozy earthy aroma permeates through the clouds, culminating in a harmonious essence. Behold, the long-awaited sunrise has arrived. As the day unfolds, a radiant aura envelops me, gradually melting away the chill and enhancing the deep, oceanic musk notes that surround me. Amidst this sensory symphony, I discern the distinct aroma of warm, moist earth mingling with the salty tang of beach sand.

My creation was supported by the exquisite blend of calone, DHM, ambroxan, and hedione.

Princess Street –A Miasma of Scents

On a bustling street in Mumbai, adjacent to Princess Street and near the Jamia Masjid, lies a fragrant world waiting to be discovered, the bustling street where the most exquisite attar purveyors can be found. From renowned international brands to those with a legacy spanning over seven decades, one can find a variety of options to indulge in. In this chapter, I shall delve deeper into these fragrances. For the moment, I would like to highlight a handful of renowned attars that are highly sought-after. The exquisite scents of majmua, shamama, oud, rhu gulab, rhu kesar, mitti and Jannat-E-Firdaus. Each one has a unique and captivating fragrance, crafted with the utmost care and precision. The interplay of notes and accords is simply divine.

Majmua, as the artisan says, took the perfumer 18 years to perfect it. Ah, Majmua…it opens up with a lush, verdant forest accord, leading into a piquant blend of hay and saffron. As it develops, notes of ripe fruit and rich soil emerge, evoking the aroma of rain on sun-warmed terracotta. The heart of the fragrance is a verdant bouquet of fruits, flowers, and hay, anchored by a base of earthy moss. Majmua evokes the velvety texture of cozy sandalwood, all while being completely devoid of any musky essence. Throughout the day, its olfactory journey is a captivating metamorphosis, unfolding from one alluring scent to the next. If I were to describe the scent, I would say that the luxurious wood is the predominant note.

It harmoniously blends various fragrances to evoke the verdant and rich essence of India's rainy season. Majmua possesses a potent aroma that may overwhelm the senses, specifically to those accustomed to Western fragrances.

Dubai Mall – Sparkling Luxury

The essence of Dubai evokes a sense of inclusivity, as if it is a fragrance that belongs to all. For me it is where perfume is everywhere in its most niche form. The Dubai Mall boasts an expansive space, and yet one floor is solely devoted to the art of perfumery. Welcome to the world of luxury, where mukhhallat invites you to indulge your olfactory senses and experience the uplifting joy of our fragrances. The crisp air in the shopping center momentarily suspends every scent in its vicinity. The stores burning exotic bakhoors and presenting their brand signatures creates a complex blend in the air, which develops a unique aura that envelopes around you and makes you feel you are in luxury. Very complex to me, but the strong notes of oud, spreading its wings, imparting a sultry woodiness, and brightening up the scene with a bouquet of roses reinforces the musk with a twist of fruitiness.

A genre of perfume characterized by smoky, sweet undertones with a hint of vanilla and a punch of dark resin. This fragrance family was previously referred to as "oriental," although more accurate and culturally appropriate terms such as "ambery" or "resinous" are now preferred. In general, the Middle-Eastern market for perfume displays a strong, cultural preference for more heavily perfumey smells.

In contrast to the conventional Indian attars that are distilled, mukhallats are a blend of culturally significant Middle-Eastern perfumery materials, including oud oil, musk, ambergris, resins, and amber accords, which are already distilled or compounded.

But the cultural and historical links between these two perfume-making cultures run deep. Arab and Persian perfumers value Indian ruhs and attars for their purity and use them to mix into their mukhallats.

العطر كالموسيقى ينقلنا إلى أزمنة أخرى..

Realm of Attars

What are attars?

The term 'attar', 'ittar,' or 'itra' is thought to have originated from the Persian word itir, which is derived from the Arabic word 'itr', signifying 'fragrance'. In England, it is called Otto, formerly called as Otter or Ottar in the 16th Century.

Ittar, the magnificent attar, is a precious elixir crafted from the purest botanical and natural sources. The wonderful essences are often obtained through the meticulous processes of hydro or steam distillation. The esteemed Persian physician Ibn Sina was the pioneer in extracting the exquisite attar of flowers through the process of distillation. Ittars, or attars, are exquisite fragrances that are typically distilled with water using natural ingredients. While it is possible to create these scents chemically, true ittars are crafted using only the finest botanicals.

These precious oils are carefully distilled and blended with a rich sandalwood base, then left to mature and develop their full potential. The maturation duration may vary from one to ten years, contingent on the chosen botanicals and the intended outcomes. The exquisite ittars are crafted through the delicate process of hydrodistillation, utilizing a still (deg) and receiving vessel (bhapka) to carefully distill the essence of flowers, herbs, spices, and other natural materials. The result is a fragrant distillate that captures the essence of nature's bounty, blended with sandalwood oil or liquid paraffins for a truly luxurious experience. The perfect methods employed at Kannauj in India continue to be utilized to this day.

Ittars are categorized according to their perceived impact on the body. Indulge in the cozy and inviting aromas of our 'warm' ittars, carefully crafted with musk, amber kesar (saffron), and shamama. Perfect for the winter season, these fragrances are believed to elevate body temperature and provide a comforting experience. In the summer season, we incorporate 'cool' ittars like rose, jasmine, khus, kewda, and mogra for their refreshing and cooling properties on the skin.

While ittars are commonly utilized as a fragrance, they also possess therapeutic and sensual properties.

With the timeline of fragrance's existence dating back to before 3000 BCE, one could argue that attars evolved during a similar era. The introduction of attars to the world is credited to the inhabitants of the Indus Valley civilization, who, alongside their counterparts in ancient Egypt and Mesopotamia, were pioneers in this regard. Encompassing a significant portion of contemporary Pakistan and India, the inhabitants of the region during that era were culturally and historically Indian. These individuals were the pioneers of the art of distillation and the production of attars. Although the term "attar" came to be used by Persian and Arab societies, its fundamental origins can be traced back to the rich cultural and taxonomic heritage of India. Interestingly, clay pots (degs) unearthed belonging to the Indus Valley civilization are almost identical to the ones used in modern-day India to produce attars.

For centuries, ittars have been revered in certain societies, precisely in Islamic cultural folklore, as a means of attracting angels and repelling malevolent spirits. Sufi saints and spiritual aspirants would adorn themselves with these scents to assist them in their journey towards enlightenment.

The different sects of Hinduism worship deities through household and temple offerings, as do Sufis in Islamic shrines and sacred khanqah's. Ittars are commonly used within the incense and food used as offerings. The ancient Hindu world boasts of texts such as Gandhasara, Gandhayukti, and Gadhashastra, which delve into the art and science of crafting cosmetics. These works make mention of the renowned Vedic noble Varahmihira's Birhat Samitha. the 77th chapter of his Brihat Samhita, entitled Gandhaukti, speaks of the "ocean of perfumes". The author enumerates a vast array of more than forty aromatic substances, which can be combined and recombined in various permutations, resulting in an astonishing 1,820 unique fragrances. He gives an interesting description of scents under sarvatobhadra, or the perfume which is good for all purposes.

His account of varying the proportions of sixteen fragrant substances and blending them reveals the advanced state-of-the-art perfumery, both natural and artificial, during his time. Gandhasara has elaborate descriptions of the methods for preparing perfumes of high quality, including the artificial ones, infusion of fragrant powders into the desired medium; digestion of aromatic materials for curing purposes; tempering or revitalizing perfumes; further intensification of scents to the required degree; and fumigation with aromatic incenses, vapors, and the like.

The Islamic texts and historical trading records provide us with insight into the earliest forms of attar production. However, it is the captivating stories from the Mughal period that offer some of the most revealing details on the subject.

The Indian attar perfumery is known for its insular approach, primarily utilizing the natural resources found within the country. In contrast, Middle Eastern oil perfumery has a wider scope, incorporating a diverse array of raw materials obtained from beyond their national boundaries. This inclination towards external sourcing can be traced back to the extensive history of Arabic-Persian empire-building and trade spanning several centuries. In the realm of Arabic oil perfumery, resins and gums reign supreme, particularly frankincense (loban/luban) and myrrh. These prized substances hold greater significance than in Indian perfumery, as they are not indigenous to India. Rather, they are cultivated and harvested in the parched, arid regions of Arabia and Africa. Some, such as copal resin, Peru, and tolu balsams, even originate from as far as Peru, Colombia, and Argentina in South America. It is worth noting that the historical and cultural connections, as well as the commercial transactions in fragrances between India and the Middle East date back to ancient times. This has resulted in a mutual transfer of resources, expertise, and even linguistic nuances pertaining to the art of perfumery across these regions.

Memoirs of Jahangir, known as Tuzk-e-Jhanangiri or Jahangir-nama, mention the itr-i-Jahangiri (so-called otto of roses). He mentions that this is a discovery that was made during his reign through the efforts of the mother of Nur-Jahan Beam. When she was making rose water, a scum formed on the surface of the dishes into which hot rose water was poured from the jugs. She meticulously gathered the scum, bit by bit. Once a substantial amount of rose water had been procured, a judicious portion of the scum was amassed. The potency of this perfume is such that a mere droplet, when applied to the palm, can fill an entire gathering with its fragrance. It is as though a multitude of crimson rosebuds have burst into bloom all at once. There is no other scent if equal excellence to it. It restored hearts that have gone and brings back withered souls. As a token of appreciation for the groundbreaking invention, he bestowed upon the inventee a magnificent string of pearls. Salima Sultan Begum was present, and she gave this oil the name of itr-i-Jahangiri.

Abul Fazal, the grand vizier of the Mughal Emperor Akbar, gave the verdict on how attar was used to making the Mabkhara incense burner. The barks that were used in Akbar's time according to Faizee were aloe, sandalwood, and cinnamon. Animal substances, such as myrrh, musk, and anbar, were used along with roots of special trees and a few other spices. The sovereign of Awadh, Ghazi-ud-Din Haidar Shah, was known to fashion fountains of ittar in the vicinity of his sleeping quarters. The perpetual operation of these fountains would imbue the surroundings with a delightful and amorous aroma, evoking a truly enchanting ambiance.

Ambergris, a crucial component of attars, boasts a rich and intricate history. The annals of Arab geographers, spanning from A.D 875 to 1165, make reference to a diverse array of anbar (Ambergirs), among them the anbar Hindi, sourced from the coasts of Basra and other locales. They mentioned the color of Anbar, which is white, black, and of dark bay color. The anbar from Hind is also known as karkbatus. Though Hind was mentioned by Arab geographers, it gathered from Indian sores or imported is unknown.

Also, in Yemen, a special variety of ittar was introduced by Arwa al-Sulayhi, the Yemeni Queen. This type of attar was prepared from mountainous flowers and given as a gift to the monarchs of Arabia.

Shamama

Shamama, also known as hina, is a meticulously crafted attar that boasts a rich blend of over sixty or more distinct aromatic ingredients, including moss, woods, cloves, ambrette seed, saffron, and sandalwood.

The precise blend of shamama is a closely-guarded mystery. The craft is not only shrouded in secrecy but also a legacy passed down for generations. The shamama fragrance has been passed down through three generations of our family and continues to be cherished by our descendants. Each distinguished perfumer family possesses a unique formula, passed down from generation to generation without any modifications. The luxurious variety of shamama attars ensures that each shamama possesses a unique aroma, distinct from any other.

Ah, the exquisite shamama attar. Its grades are as varied as the fragrant raw materials used to distill it. Some are distilled purely from sandalwood, while others are crafted from a blend of synthetic sandalore and bacdanol, with sandalwood as the base ingredient. The quality and quantity of these ingredients determine the unique character of each shamama attar.

Our exquisite shamama attar is crafted with a harmonious blend of over seventy all-natural ingredients, including the finest valerian, spikenard, kapur kachari, saffron, charila, cardamom, juniper berry, nutmeg, mace, clove bud, ambrette seed, and sandalwood. It is a fragrant composition that can be nuanced or enhanced in an endless array of possibilities. In this modern era of affordable synthetic alternatives, the once revered craft of attar-making has dwindled, leaving only a select few families who continue to produce shamama using traditional methods. The contemporary shamama attars available in the market are a fusion of synthetic and natural elements, resulting in a surprisingly delightful aroma.

The art of attars is a personal journey, where each perfumer selects the notes that resonate with their unique vision, resulting in a signature scent that is entirely their own. This craft demands a lifetime to master and ultimately develop a unique essence that can be marketed.

The traditional technique of extracting shamama attar is a fascinating process worth exploring. Crafting a multi-faceted fragrance is a meticulous and intricate process that demands great effort and time. A single composition requires a minimum of forty-five days to reach its full potential. Crafting a shamama attar involves a meticulous process consisting of two major steps. Attars are crafted through a careful distillation process in copper vessels, carefully divided into stages using the Deg-Bhapka method, as well as the One-pot Cooking technique, known as Patila Pakana. The distillation process should done only in copper vessels as copper is the best conductor of heat which has even distribution of heat. The exquisite Chonga condenser is crafted from the finest bamboo, lending a touch of natural elegance to your olfactory experience. Our fragrance is crafted with the warmth of a crackling wood fire, using only the finest forest wood for an authentic and natural aroma.

In the creation of shamama, every element is cherished. The water is recycled and the leftover ingredients after distillation are carefully sun-dried and utilized in the crafting of incense sticks or Bakhoor.

During the daily distillation process, it is recommended to keep the Bhapka (collecting vessel) tilted and secured to the wall. This allows for the removal of excess water and creates ample space for the next day's infusion of ingredients. This process allows for the oil to infuse and blend within the Bhapka, enhancing its fragrance. The aqueous extract is reintroduced into the Deg vessel.

At the initial phase, we carefully distill charila, a delicate lichen found on rocks in the Himalayan woods. This exquisite ingredient exudes a bitter, mossy fragrance reminiscent of oakmoss. Charila is meticulously charged in the Deg, half full with clean water, best if soaked overnight, and then, using the traditional method of hydro-distillation, expertly infused with the rich and luxurious aroma of sandalwood oil over the course of ten days.

In the second phase, we carefully distill a blend of finely ground and delicately roasted botanicals, roots, and aromatic plants. This unique combination includes rare ingredients, such as spikenard, valerian root, Cyperus root, and sugandh kokila, which may not be familiar to the Western olfactory senses. From the initial phase, the aromatic essences are distilled into the sandalwood oil, which exudes a fragrance reminiscent of a luxurious monument. This is sustained for a fortnight.

Incorporating choya is the third step in the process. Ah, the exquisite shamama fragrance is crafted with a blend of three distinct choya varieties. The selection and timing of usage is at the discretion of the perfumer. The aim is to incorporate a rich, smoky leather note into shamama. Choya nakh is a smoky and alluring fragrance that captures the essence of charred seashells. These shells are carefully roasted and smoked over a dry fire in a sand pit before being macerated and cooked gently in sandalwood oil, resulting in a rich and complex aroma. Choya loban is a precious essence obtained through the dry distillation of frankincense resin. The liquid tears of resin are carefully collected from the heated Degs or directed into a receiving vessel. Choya ral is a complex and alluring fragrance, crafted from the resin of the sal tree through a meticulous dry distillation process. It emanates a rich, balsamic scent with sweet and smoky notes, evoking a sense of sophistication and mystery. The loban is delicately infused in the final stages of the One-pot cooking process, while the choya nakh is carefully incorporated into the Deg.

Occasionally, a touch of essence is delicately infused into the Bhapka from the very beginning to achieve a unique and memorable aroma. In our process, we delicately infuse the essence of seashells, which have been carefully prepared by cleaning, roasting, and powdering, in a muslin cloth bag. The vapors are then allowed to gracefully mingle with the intoxicating sandalwood oil in our Bhapka, which is already enriched with the alluring scents of moss and other aromatic ingredients.

In the fourth phase, we carefully distill a blend of aromatic spices and herbs. A new batch of aromatic cardamom, exotic mace, rich nutmeg, warm clove, and musky ambrette seeds are carefully placed into the patila. The wonderful essence of shamama is delicately infused into the heart, simmering on low heat. The exquisite essence of the patila is meticulously guarded and attentively observed as we approach the final stages of perfecting its signature aroma.

In the ultimate phase, we blend the exquisite shamama attar with pre-distilled attars like the alluring rose, enchanting jasmine, fragrant kewra, exotic champaca, and precious saffron. In the final stages, we incorporate additional aromatic elements like rose hydrosols, musk grains, and precious ambergris tinctures or oud. This exquisite blend is then left to infuse in a tightly sealed vessel (patila) over a gentle flame for a full day. Once the mixture has been meticulously skimmed for absolute clarity, it is carefully decanted into leather caskets to mature and harmonize.

Shamama attars possess a unique blend of characteristics that make them stand out. They offer earthy and vetiver notes, accompanied by a pungent saffron or henna scent with hints of hay. The heart of these attars is rich and ambery-aromatic, while also featuring animalic facets that mimic the texture and scent of ambergris, civet, heavy musk, and Hindi oud. Finally, the base notes are tenacious and reminiscent of moss, wood, baked earth, and tea leaves.

Simple combinations of ingredients to create a shamama.

Charilla	60	Foundation
Nagarmotha	30	Heart
Jatamansi	30	Heart
Kapur Kachri	10	Heart
Sugandh Bala	2	Heart
Sugandh Kokila	2	Heart
Sugandh Mantri	2	Heart
Cardamom	0.5	Heart
Clove	0.5	Heart
Nutmeg	0.2	Heart
Mace	0.2	Heart
Saffron	0.5	Heart
Attar Gulab	5	Top
Attar Kewra	3	Top
Attar Motia	2	Top
Attar Mehndi	1	Top
Choya Nakh	1	Top
Oudh	0.1	Top

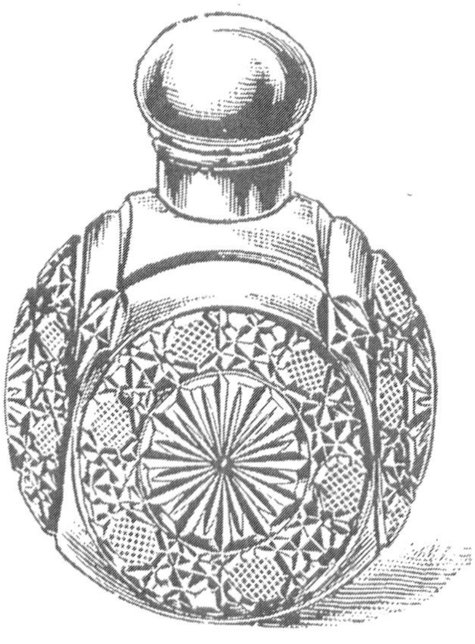

Eau de You

How to choose a Fragrance for yourself?

Indulge in the sensory experience of selecting a scent that speaks to your unique essence. Allow your olfactory senses to guide you towards a fragrance that harmonizes with your personal style and evokes your desired mood.

The art of selecting a scent, whether for oneself or another, can prove to be quite a challenge. Fragrance selection is a highly personal and revealing choice that can reflect one's unique style and grooming habits, ultimately leaving a lasting impression on those around them. Your persona is not only visually perceived, but also unconsciously sensed through the power of fragrance. As you approach others, they will come to realize your essence through their olfactory senses. Before delving into the process of selecting a fragrance, it is important to understand that the essence of wearing a scent is to enhance one's allure and adorn one's refined appearance.

The first step in selecting a fragrance is to possess a fundamental understanding of the primary scent families in perfumery. These include citrus, floral, fruity, musky, woody, and ambery, as I have previously discussed in my earlier chapters. One need not embark on a lengthy scientific journey to create fragrances. Instead, consider exploring your garden, nearby hypermarket, or even your own kitchen. The essence surrounds you. The art lies in arranging these elements in your environment according to their olfactory families, thereby defining the fragrance and its family. Perfumery is an art that is highly subjective, but every creation must have a starting point.

Indulge in the art of olfactory exploration by identifying various aromatic components in your environment and categorizing them into distinct fragrance families. As you inhale their essence, committing it to memory will undoubtedly prove beneficial. I have provided a selection of exquisite ingredients to begin your olfactory journey, with the option to expand your repertoire as your passion for perfumery grows.

Citrus: Experience the vibrant essence of freshly squeezed lemon or the zesty aroma of ripe orange pulp.

Floral: Experience the essence of a crimson rose and the alluring aroma of jasmine as you delicately crush their petals between your palms. The essence of a blooming garden will be carried by the florist.

Fruity: Indulge in the lusciousness of freshly sliced apple, juicy watermelon, and succulent strawberry for a fruity sensation that tantalizes the senses.

Spicy: Indulge in the aromatic notes of black pepper, cardamom, and ginger. Craft your own unique fragrance as you prepare your morning masala chai.

Woody: Experience the woody aroma of freshly sharpened pencils, reminiscent of a cozy study lined with bookshelves.

Green: Experience the freshness of nature by extracting the essence of green grass twigs crushed delicately between your fingertips. The verdant aroma of freshly cut grass is classified as a green fragrance.

Leathery: Indulge in the luxurious aroma of supple leather as you recline in the driver's seat of a sleek automobile.

Ambery: Indulge in the warm and inviting aroma of ambery notes by simply taking a hardcover book from the library and inhaling its pages. The alluring aroma of moist, cozy, and shadowy pages evokes the essence of amber, albeit not precisely.

Musky: A challenging fragrance to capture, but one can indulge in the warm, musky aroma emanating from the fur of our beloved pets.

Aldehydic: Experience the aldehydic notes reminiscent of freshly cleaned floors and laundry with a subtle yet invigorating aroma. Aldehydes impart a sense of cleanliness.

Sweet: Indulge in the saccharine aroma of a homemade sugar syrup or savor the sweet scents of jaggery, fennel, and vanilla beans.

After spending some time, perhaps a week or so, you will gain a deeper understanding of fragrance families, which will aid you in defining any scent. Indulge in the art of fragrance selection by selecting your preferred olfactory family.

The second step in crafting your olfactory journey is to understand the intention behind your desire for a fragrance or scented creation. Understanding the motive is of utmost significance. The selection of a fragrance is a deeply personal and artistic decision, as it is influenced by one's emotional state and individual perspective. Our aim is to simplify your fragrance selection process for a more enjoyable purchasing experience. Simplification can be achieved by defining the following points according to your own preferences.

Is this fragrance intended for a gentleman or a lady? In the contemporary era, it has become effortless for fragrance houses and digital marketplaces to classify their offerings into distinct masculine and feminine categories.

Imagine yourself wearing this fragrance to various destinations - the office, a night party, family gatherings, festivals, the shopping mall, the airport, the railway station, the gym, outdoor sports, a house party, or simply relaxing at home. It is essential to consider the population of individuals in the vicinity of where you intend to wear your fragrance. In the midst of a bustling crowd, a powerful and blossoming fragrance may be necessary to combat the various levels of surrounding scents. At home, one may opt for a subtle fragrance to create a comfortable atmosphere for others.

What is the desired time of day for wearing? Perhaps all day, or solely during the evening. The olfactory principle is to capture the essence of the ambient temperature. The crispness of early morning and late evening is a refreshing contrast to the warmth of the daytime. In elevated temperatures, the aroma may not endure on your garments or skin, whereas during the evening, it flourishes. For daytime wear, I would recommend selecting an Eau de Parfum, while an Eau de Toilette would be more suitable for evening occasions. The concentration of a fragrance is elevated in an Eau de Parfum compared to an Eau de Toilette, resulting in better longevity of the scent at elevated temperatures. Brands today mention about fragrances are if classified as Eau de Parfum (EDP) or Eau de Toilette (EDT). Attars, with their high concentration, are able to withstand even the most extreme temperatures.

The consideration of budget is of utmost importance from the outset, as we are aware that the acquisition of fragrance can be either a lavish indulgence or a necessity. By determining your budget, you can effortlessly curate a selection of options within that price range. The olfactory universe is vast, and one can easily lose oneself amidst the plethora of brands. One may find it challenging to discern all the fragrances displayed on the shelf, leading to a potential state of confusion.

When selecting a fragrance, it is essential to consider one's preferred style or attire. This fragrance has the versatility to suit any occasion, whether it be a classic and refined setting or a more relaxed and informal atmosphere. The olfactory experience is a personal one, as you are the best judge of your own preferences. As a perfumer, one must consider what facets of their essence they wish to accentuate through their attire. If you desire to accentuate the opulence of your ensemble - be it jewelry, suit, scarf, accessory, or the like - I recommend perusing our selection of niche and global classic brands. Niche fragrances and global classics are crafted with exquisite ingredients, inspired by a profound artistic vision, and leave a lasting impression. If you desire to accentuate your refined and polished appearance, consider selecting from our top-selling fragrances of the year, which exude a contemporary and sophisticated aura. Contemporary fragrances boast a harmonious fragrance structure, while their classic counterparts tend to be more anchored in their base notes. For a more understated look that harmonizes with your environment, opt for a fragrance with delicate powdery or creamy notes. Several brand collections boasts a plethora of fragrances that are green, clean, and sustainable - perfect for those seeking to embody simplicity.

The third phase involves olfactory evaluation. One must experience the fragrance firsthand through olfactory senses before making a purchase. Once your olfactory preferences are well defined, you shall select no more than 4 to 5 fragrances from the array. Firstly, it is essential to experience each fragrance on a paper blotter. Take in each scent individually and then narrow down your selection to two final fragrances. Experience the final two fragrances by applying them delicately on your wrists or forearms and assess their essence. When selecting, one must follow the thumb rule of shortlisting.

Discovering the olfactory family that resonates with your senses is the cornerstone of a fragrance's signature, one that permeates throughout its top and base notes. The essence of your fragrance should revolve around your personal preferences.

Upon application to your forearms, swiftly inhale to capture the top notes. Allow a brief intermission of approximately one minute before inhaling once more to detect the middle notes. After a pause of 15 minutes, observe how the fragrance progresses towards the base note. After a few hours, one may experience the lingering essence of the fragrance.

One may occasionally experience a fleeting olfactory sensation. This is due to the fact that each individual possesses a distinct biological composition, resulting in a unique skin texture and functionality. The unique biology of your skin plays a crucial role in the absorption and diffusion of fragrance. For those with dry skin, it is recommended to first hydrate the skin with a lotion before applying fragrance. However, for those with oily skin, it is best to avoid oily creams and lotions before applying a fragrance. It is also advised to avoid applying any lotion on the area where you plan to spray the fragrance.

I believe that selecting a fragrance requires careful consideration. While there are numerous methods suggested by experts, I recommend keeping a few key pointers in mind. These may be based on external factors or personal preferences, but they will undoubtedly aid in narrowing down the vast array of scents available in today's market.

It is important to inquire about the purpose of your fragrance purchase when visiting a shop. It is effortless for them to showcase the finest in their boutique.

When selecting an itr, consider the fragrance notes that appeal to your senses and the occasion for which you will be wearing it.

Selecting an itr requires an approach akin to that of a perfumer.

It is essential to understand the narrative, the heritage, and the perfumer's methodology that led to its inception. Please do not hesitate to share your budget, as attars typically begin at higher price points. However, considering their formulation, they exhibit remarkable longevity and potent sillage. The end result is a worthy investment.

When selecting an itr, it is essential to consider two fundamental factors:

Select the atmospheric ambiance that best complements your desired fragrance experience from a collection of scents inspired by the seasons: summer, rainy, winters, and more. Each attar exhibits unique characteristics depending on the prevailing climate. Shamama is a delightful winter fragrance, while oud is a versatile scent that can be enjoyed year-round.

May I inquire about the occasion for which you seek a fragrance? Would this fragrance be more suitable for everyday use or reserved for special events?

The rich heritage of attars is steeped in mystery, with their origins shrouded in secrecy. To truly appreciate the nuances of each unique blend, one must take the time to immerse themselves in the fragrance. A visit to a fragrance shop will allow you to explore the intricacies of each attar, as you delicately apply it to your wrists and allow it to evolve over the course of 4-5 hours. Only then can you make an informed decision on which attar to add to your collection. It is recommended to refrain from applying them onto white garments, as it may result in staining. These fragrances can be delicately applied to your hair, skin, or even the interior of your purse. You may also choose to apply them to a cotton swab and place it in your wardrobe for a subtle and alluring scent. As you inhale the attar, allow the fragrance to transport you to a world of rich storytelling and captivating history, fully immersing yourself in its essence.

In my professional opinion, attars exude a timeless and opulent essence that surpasses any other perfume format. Their presence throughout the ages only adds to their undeniable allure.

There are two distinct categories. The first is our Pure Singulars, which are crafted using a single process and remain unblended for a pure and unadulterated fragrance experience.

Secondly, exquisite Mukhallats are crafted from a harmonious blend of carefully selected natural oils and attars.

Indulging in the essence of pure attars, such as shamama, mitti, gulab, khus, and others can be quite a luxurious experience. To fully savor their exquisite aroma, one may consider the following two methods:

The layering technique involves delicately applying a small amount of pure attar before spritzing on your favorite perfume or mukhallat, resulting in an intensified and alluring fragrance.

Indulge in a luxurious bathing experience by adding a drop of this exquisite attar to your bath and shower routine. After bathing, apply it once more on your wrist or pair it with a mukhallat or perfume to elevate its alluring effects.

One must intimately experience them to discern the perfect match. Once you have curated a selection, procure petite amounts and allow them to develop over several weeks. Then, select the one that most pleases your senses. Patience is key in discovering the perfect match for your body's natural scent.

As attars are crafted with care, they demand an equal measure of care and affection to truly appreciate their essence.

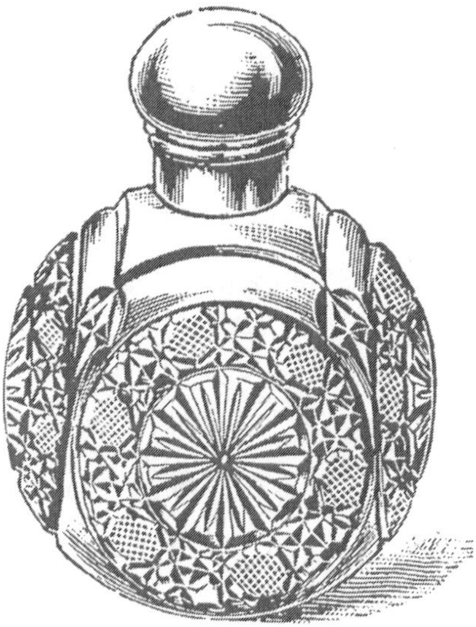

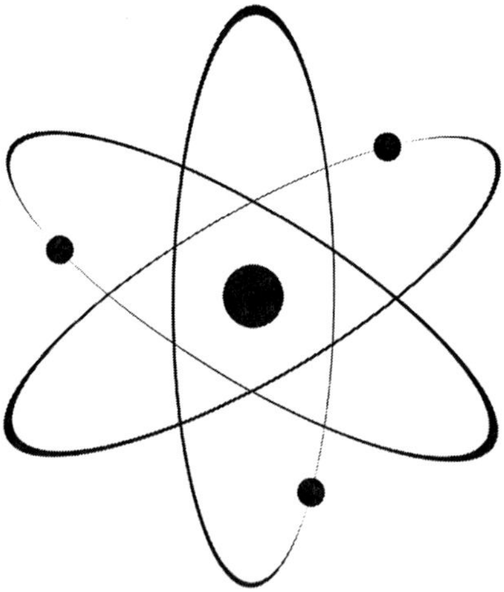

The Aroma of Tomorrow

Exploring Innovative Applications and Technologies

The art of fragrance has forever been intertwined with the enchantment of elevating our sensory encounters, evoking profound emotions, and creating indelible imprints upon our memories. Within this chapter, we shall embark upon a captivating exploration of two alluring facets that grace the realm of perfumery. First and foremost, let us embark on a fragrant journey, delving into the myriad possibilities of a scent's enchanting allure across diverse worlds, be it the realm of corporate identity or the world of captivating event ambiance. In our quest, we will dive into the where the harmonious fusion of cutting-edge technologies, such as artificial intelligence, quantum biology, and neuromarketing intertwine to redefine the very essence of fragrance experimentation and personalization.

The next wave of fragrance applications

I have forever been fascinated with the art of shopping, for it is a delightful voyage of discovery. Window shopping, in particular, has become an integral part of my explorations, where I seek to unearth novel inspirations. It is a world where colors dance harmoniously, forms captivate the senses, advertisements weave tales of allure, branding displays exude sophistication, and products invite with their irresistible charm. Let us participate in a fragrant drive, where the ethereal essence of companies, departments, retail stores, and kiosks intertwines with the very fabric of their brand identities. We have the power to imbue their physical spaces with the essence of fragrance, or even adorn their employees' attire and business cards with aromatic allure. By doing so, businesses can craft a captivating multisensory journey that lingers in the memories of their esteemed clients and cherished customers. In the domain of olfactory artistry, it is a delightful notion to imagine the grandeur of larger industries like inside of malls adorning themselves with their own signature, meticulously crafted to leave a lasting impression in the hearts of their esteemed visitors.

Hotels are those wonderful sanctuaries that attract us with their charm and invite us to embark on a sensory journey with our beloved family, cherished friends, or esteemed colleagues. Whether it be for joyous celebrations or a solitary retreat, these opulent oases provide the perfect backdrop for indulging in moments of self-discovery and blissful solitude. I am cognizant that select luxury hotels possess their own distinctive fragrance, often unveiled upon one's arrival. However, hotels possess the potential to elevate their guests' experiences by curating an array of diverse and unparalleled olfactory atmospheres. Crafted with meticulous attention to detail, these olfactory masterpieces have been artfully designed to cater to various spaces, whether it be the grand lobbies, serene spas, bustling business rooms, or the cozy guest rooms. Each fragrance can be carefully curated to elevate the ambience and transport our cherished guests on an unforgettable sensory odyssey. These exquisite fragrances can also be meticulously crafted into bespoke collections, designed to envelop discerning individuals in an aura of elegance and sophistication. Perfectly suited for the most exclusive occasions such as weddings, birthday soirées, or any momentous celebration, these scents will transport you to a realm of unparalleled olfactory delights.

Imagine the wonderful artistry of tailoring the olfactory symphony within your vehicle, harmonizing it effortlessly with every occasion or mood. Like a gentle breeze caressing the senses, personalized fragrances have the power to elevate every moment of your journey. Whether embarking on a romantic evening drive, a delightful family outing, or a captivating social gathering, these olfactory masterpieces have the ability to weave an enchanting tapestry of scents, forging an intimate bond between individuals and their cherished vehicles. Imagine a wondrous creation, a marvel of technology that possesses the power to transform the very ambiance within your vehicle. Inspired by the intricate algorithms of weather patterns and the art of mood enhancement, this extraordinary device delicately disperses the perfect dosage of amazing perfume, enveloping your journey in an enchanting aura of pure delight.

Events can be beautifully enhanced by intertwining the ethereal essence of fragrance within the very fabric of decor and attire. The artful arrangement of fragrances can effortlessly conjure distinct emotions or elevate the essence of an occasion, crafting a captivating symphony for those in attendance. Enveloped in the invisible essence of scented floral arrangements, one is transported to a realm were fragranced fabrics dance in harmonious synchrony. The boundless possibilities of olfactory delight unfold, inviting one to embark on a sensory journey beyond imagination.

The cutting-edge technologies transforming the world of fragrances

The world has undergone a complete revolution, and with it, the advent of artificial intelligence has been bestowed upon us. The emergence of AI has not only facilitated our research and productivity but also ushered in novel possibilities for numerous industries. Presently, there exist professionals who possess certified qualifications in the fields of AI and machine learning.

Fifteen years have passed since I first crafted my own software on C++. At that moment, I persistently queried the agency responsible for my software as to why an automated response or calibration of my formulations could not be implemented. I even attempted to perform the task on my Excel spreadsheets to ascertain its feasibility. It took me half a decade to formulate adequate responses. Due to my lack of formal education in the realm of IT, I was unable to yield the desired outcomes. However, during this time, our global perfumery industry had successfully implemented AI-based platforms to strengthen their creative endeavors.

The realm of perfumery remains one in which artificial intelligence falls short, for the intricacies of crafting a precise formula demand the discerning touch of a human nose, steeped in the art and science of fragrance. Inevitably, scents are intended for the consumption of mankind, and each individual possesses their own unique predilections and aversions. Even the creations of the human nose are subject to discrimination, as each nose possesses a unique ability to design based on its individual experiences and years of learning.

I experimented with a method that proved successful within the confines of my laboratory. As I perused the archives of my digital memory, I chanced upon a series of breathtaking photographs. My mind was immediately seized by the notion of harnessing the power of artificial intelligence to recreate this stunning vista. The notion occurred to me that a color palette might be a viable approach to consider. I perused the vast expanse of the internet in search of an artificial intelligence capable of extracting the most prominent hues from a given image. The tool successfully extracted a total of twelve distinct colors from the uploaded image, each of which proved to be the most prominent hues present within the composition. One may ponder the reason why colors have been chosen. Extensive research has been conducted on the relationship between color and fragrance, revealing a correlation between olfactive families and hues. The color green is often associated with the verdant hues of the natural world, while blue is commonly linked to the vast expanses of the ocean or other aquatic environments. With the aid of this tool, I can expedite the process of concocting an original fragrance. After obtaining the colors, I meticulously recorded the key families and corresponding ingredients that they represent. Through this process, I was able to develop a detailed formula.

In my experience with AI, I have discovered that it is a remarkable tool for expediting the creative process. By providing a more precise and detailed roadmap for developing new creations and aligning them with established standards, AI can greatly enhance the efficiency and effectiveness of one's work.

Though the journey ahead is lengthy, I remain confident that we shall arrive at our destination. Yet, one cannot help but ponder: is it feasible to construct a comprehensive formula solely through the input of textual passages, visual imagery, auditory recordings, and prevailing patterns? The formula in question is one that is imbued with both scientific and artistic equilibrium. The answer to this question remains elusive, and yet, undoubtedly, there are those who are diligently pursuing it.

The mysterious realm of fragrance, with its ethereal allure, remains shrouded in uncertainty, defying our feeble attempts to foretell its destiny. Yet, undeterred by this enigmatic nature, diligent researchers have embarked upon a profound odyssey, delving into the profound depths of knowledge, forging complex relationships between diverse scientific disciplines. Their tireless endeavors seek to unveil a fresh vantage point, a veritable panacea that shall propel this artistic endeavor to unprecedented heights. The realm of quantum biology, under the guidance of our esteemed scientific community, has bestowed upon us a fresh perspective, enabling us to delve deeper into the intricate workings of olfaction. In contemplating the essence of existence, one cannot deny the pervasive nature of energy. Indeed, when we perceive the constituents of our surroundings as ethereal vibrations, imbued with captivating fragrances, they possess an enigmatic allure. Such aromatic energies possess the remarkable ability to bestow upon us a sense of delight, as they traverse the ethereal realm, transcending from one human being to another. Frequently, I find myself pondering the possibility of transposing fragrances from one locale to another, guided by the profound insights of quantum biology. Alternatively, I contemplate the exploration of novel energies that may yield fresh ingredients resonating at frequencies capable of establishing a profound connection with our subconscious minds, thereby evoking a profound sense of self-awareness. The exploration of conscious and unconscious decision making remains an ongoing endeavor within the realm of neuroconsumer science, a field in which learned scholars have meticulously delineated the intricacies involved. Neuromarketing, heralded as the vanguard of marketing, represents a paradigm shift in comprehending the intricacies of human cognition and decision-making processes. The ethereal essence of fragrance possesses a remarkable ability to not only guide our decision-making processes but also bridge the chasms that exist within diverse industries. By merging the realms of quantum biology and neuromarketing, one can anticipate the possibility of crafting fragrances or molecules that possess the remarkable ability to enhance and redefine personalities, industries, and applications.

In today's vibrant digital landscape, a plethora of companies have emerged, offering an abundance of phone apps, websites, and other innovative platforms. These extraordinary avenues not only allow you to select a fragrance that resonates with your unique essence but also empower you to embark on an artistic journey of crafting your very own olfactory masterpiece. The possibilities are boundless as you immerse yourself in a world of limitless creativity and self-expression. As you embark on a delightful journey through our carefully curated platforms, you will have the pleasure of handpicking the inputs that resonate with your discerning taste. The meticulously crafted algorithms, tailored exclusively by each esteemed company, proceed to weave their magic, artfully blending and harmonizing the chosen inputs or illustrations. The result? A bespoke fragrance that encapsulates your individuality and desires, a sensory masterpiece crafted just for you. Behold, a myriad of avant-garde methods for the artistry of bespoke perfumery and beyond. The art of mixing, or as we creatively refer to it, blending, is a harmonious dance of creating equilibrium. Balancing, is the ultimate test that each unique soul must face, and indeed, it requires a generous investment of time. Artificial intelligence, with its remarkable capabilities, has successfully bridged the divide between attaining a harmonious solution and doing so within a significantly compressed timeframe. In my quest for innovation and excellence, I find myself standing at the precipice of a new level of artistic mastery. The time has come to embark on a journey of refinement, to delve deeper into the very essence of fragrance creation. The mission is clear: to unravel the intricacies, to unravel the complexities that lie in the heart of this olfactory art form. With unwavering determination, we shall forge ahead, armed with our passion and expertise, to distil the formula to its purest form. The path may be arduous, but the rewards shall be unparalleled. Let us embrace this challenge with open hearts and open minds, for it is through this process that we shall unlock the true potential of fragrance creation. In my humble perspective, the notion of offering a creatively innovative resolution within a condensed timeframe holds immense potential as a remarkable marketing tactic. However, the crux lies in the art of meticulously tailoring each masterpiece to suit the unique preferences of every individual, while simultaneously minimizing the need for excessive inputs or prolonged screen engagement. Naturally, the ethereal essence of fragrance remains elusive until a tangible sample is crafted. However, envisioning the aromatic image, immersing oneself in its olfactory essence, and experiencing the invisible aura it imparts upon one's being would undoubtedly be a delightful indulgence in the art of personal creation. Imagine the sheer magic of crafting a musical note, delicately woven from the very essence of the ingredients you have thoughtfully selected. This exquisite creation, unique to your vision, shall be accompanied by an elegant bottle, bearing the mark of your personal touch. And to complete this symphony of artistry, a name, resonating with the essence of your creation, shall be bestowed upon it. Embrace the boundless possibilities of your imagination, and let your creativity compose a masterpiece that shall leave a lasting impression. In the realm of artistic innovation, envision a harmonious fusion of aromatic elements, melodious symphonies, vibrant hues, exquisite bottles, immersive virtual realms, and meticulously curated fragrance essences. This captivating amalgamation shall undoubtedly pose as the next frontier for the ever-evolving AI domain.

At the heart of every development lies the exquisite art of personalized briefing and the harmonious exchange of ideas between our esteemed clients and the visionary perfumery houses. Crafting an exquisite olfactory masterpiece necessitates the presence of a meticulously articulated brief. However, the pursuit of a flawless brief is perpetually an exhilarating endeavor. Once the captivating brief is artfully shared, the visionary creative team within the illustrious industry embark on a mesmerizing journey of data exploration, seamlessly blending the realms of analysis, prediction, and meticulous recordings. With an exquisite touch, they delicately calibrate the data, harmonizing its intricate nuances to craft a fragrance that transcends mere acceptance and instead evokes a profound sense of admiration and allure. Creating something truly remarkable and extraordinary demands an investment of countless hours, a relentless pursuit of excellence, and a profound mastery of one's craft. It necessitates the accumulation of wisdom, honing of skills, and a deep reservoir of expertise that can only be acquired through years of dedicated effort. Undoubtedly, the presence of humans is an absolute necessity to infuse that exquisite sense of equilibrium and a distinctive essence into every fragrance, rendering it utterly irreplaceable. However, let us envision a solution that transcends the limitations of manual briefing and comprehending the intricacies of diverse data analysis. In the realm of modern business, visionary companies are diligently crafting exceptional platforms that effortlessly streamline the process of consumer or client briefing. These ingenious solutions are meticulously designed, drawing upon a wealth of meticulously analyzed data accumulated over years of tireless research. By seamlessly amalgamating their extensive reservoir of knowledge and insights, today's companies have ingeniously devised a means to address any given brief with unparalleled efficiency and precision. In my humble opinion, there exists a vast realm of untapped potential when it comes to expressing the essence of individuality through the art of scent. By delving deeper into the realms of creativity, we can elevate the very concept of personalized fragrances to unprecedented heights, captivating the senses and leaving an indelible mark on all who encounter them. Imagine a world where the power of self-expression is encapsulated in the ethereal realm of scent. Picture this: effortlessly, one can effortlessly convey their essence through the artistry of fragrance. Whether it be a few carefully chosen words or a captivating visual, the possibilities are endless. With a mere upload of a picture, a glimpse into one's soul, or a cherished memory, a transformative journey begins. In this realm of boundless creativity, the brief is the catalyst, igniting the imagination and guiding the path towards a truly unique olfactory masterpiece. But it doesn't end there. The alchemy of expertise takes center stage as skilled perfumers delicately refine the creative formula, weaving together the threads of inspiration and personal choice. And here, dear connoisseur of the extraordinary, lies the pièce de résistance - the signature. A moment of pure individuality, where the consumer's discerning taste and desires converge, leaving an indelible mark on their bespoke fragrance. The symphony of scents harmonizes with the essence of self, creating an olfactory masterpiece that is truly one-of-a-kind. Welcome to a world where creativity knows no bounds, where fragrance becomes a canvas for self-expression, and where the art of perfumery transcends the ordinary. Embrace the extraordinary, for your journey awaits. By harnessing the cutting-edge realms of neuroscience, quantum biology, and their related domains, we are embarking on a journey that opens up boundless possibilities for the world. Through meticulous refinement of data, we aim to unravel the intricate tapestry of consumer and client inputs, enabling us to deliver unparalleled creative solutions. This pursuit not only promises to unlock innovative olfactive accords, but also unveils uncharted dimensions and profiles, paving the way for groundbreaking inventions.

As we embark on a captivating journey into the realm of fragrance, it becomes abundantly clear that the horizons are brimming with boundless possibilities, beckoning us to indulge in their alluring charm. Embracing the art of scent infusion across a myriad of industries and environments, the fragrance industry is poised to embark on a remarkable metamorphosis. By harnessing the power of cutting-edge AI, neuroscience, neuromarketing, quantum biology, and such technologies, a realm of personalized exploration and exquisite recommendations awaits. Brace yourself for an extraordinary olfactory journey as the fragrance industry transcends boundaries and enters a new era of innovation. Through a harmonious fusion of forward-thinking and the boundless possibilities offered by cutting-edge technology, we have the extraordinary ability to unlock uncharted realms of sensory encounters. These awe-inspiring experiences have the power to etch themselves into the very fabric of our existence, forever transforming the way we perceive and engage with the world around us. The realm of fragrance in the future is an exhilarating domain brimming with boundless possibilities, where the harmonious fusion of artistic ingenuity and cutting-edge technology shall revolutionize our sensory odysseys.

Evolving Echoes

In the realm of perfumery, our pursuit of knowledge and the weight of our heritage are eternal. The journey we embark upon in this enchanting world of scents knows no bounds. It is our sacred duty, should we not already be compelled, to impart this wisdom to the next generation, ensuring the legacy of fragrance endures in all its splendor. It shall forever linger as a profound olfactory imprint within the fabric of my cherished memories, evoking the essence of two exciting events that have adorned my existence. In the enchanting year of 2023, I was myself immersed in my aromatic piano, where the delicate dance of scents unfolded. It was then that my beloved daughter, Vedanti, graced me with her presence, her magical spirit creating a spark of inspiration within my soul. She expressed a whimsical desire, a longing for a fragrance that would encapsulate her very essence, a fragrant symphony crafted exclusively for her. She graciously requested that I bring upon her a selection of exquisite raw materials, from which she aspires to craft her very own olfactory masterpiece. I provided her with delicate smelling strips, gracefully immersed in the enchanting essences of Bergamot, Galaxolide, and Patchouli. She eloquently portrayed them as exquisite essences that bring a sense of invigorating vitality and radiant luminosity. As her artistic inspiration blossomed over time, she graciously divulged the precise proportions to harmoniously blend these aromatic treasures. To my delight, she expressed her desire to craft a fragrance that captures the essence of summer. She graciously requested that I assist in skillfully blending the vibrant notes of Bergamot and the alluring allure of Galaxolide, while delicately infusing subtle traces of Patchouly to add a touch of intrigue. On my discussion with her on the reasoning behind such a choice, and she artfully elucidated that patchouli, with its weighty essence and natural woody aroma, serves to reinforce the inherent freshness of citrus. Furthermore, she explained upon the captivating allure of Galaxolide, its lingering and transparent nature, which adds a captivating dimension to the already intriguing Bergamot. In the sphere of my initial musings, I perceived her as an archer, letting go her arrows into the obscurity of the night, merely indulging in her imaginative pursuits. However, as a profound epiphany dawned upon me, founded myself swelling with pride, for she possesses the olfactory acumen that may one day lead her to continue our esteemed legacy. In all honesty, words fail to capture the sheer elation that overwhelmed me, as my rosy cheeks transformed into glistening pools of emotion.

In the dreamy evening of Shanghai's waning winter, we found ourselves ensconced within the opulent embrace of a bustling mall. As we embarked upon our journey of shopping, my beloved Anvikka, her tiny hand entwined with mine, was suddenly seized by an irresistible allure. With an impulsive grace, she darted towards a starry beauty counter, nestled amidst the vibrant tapestry of the mall's grandeur. We imagined hues and beauty captivating her gaze, yet to our astonishment, she instead gravitated towards a resplendent perfume exhibit. With grace, she delicately plucked a scented strip, bringing it closer to her nose, indulging in its aromatic allure. The charming lady gave her yet another delicate strip, topped with the floating essence of perfume. And as the first word escaped her lips, it danced upon the air like a fragrant blossom - "Flower". A symphony of scents would have unfolded, revealing the harmonious beauty that graced her senses as she said it is Nice. In the delicate realm of scents, realizing myself momentarily perplexed, as if a whisper had eluded my senses. With a gentle curiosity, I inquired of her, "Please tell, what fragrant essence did you perceive?" She described it as a lot of flowers. It has been a delightful passage of time since that enchanting occasion, and she now finds herself irresistibly drawn to the allure of perfume counters, where she graciously requests to sample the delicate strips of olfactory delight. In the comfort of her own abode, she indulges in the aromatic exploration of scented candles, gracefully discerning the intricate notes that dance within. In fact, she astutely identifies fragrances she has acquired knowledge of, such as the tantalizing scent of freshly popped popcorn, with an air of sophistication and finesse. It is truly invigorating when she unveils her innate brilliance, crafting her own vocabulary at such a tender age. In the realm of her nascent aspirations, it is premature to ponder the path that awaits her. However, one cannot deny the celestial endowment given upon her olfactory senses, as well as her discovering intellect.

I have always held the belief that a well-crafted scent will inevitably discover its rightful home. The essence of goodness is often open to interpretation, but a harmonious blend of carefully curated notes, skillfully crafted, and with a distinctive character can be deemed a fine fragrance.

A fragrance is a hidden allure, a romance waiting to be discovered. Its realization is an internal journey of understanding and adapting to its essence. The sense of romance that a fragrance evokes is simply breathtaking. The essence of fragrance intertwines harmoniously with the ethereal essence of the human soul. Across the annals of time, a myriad of illustrious civilizations have gracefully intertwined aromatic tributes within the sacred tapestry of their divine and ethereal rituals. From the ethereal essence of incense in the sacred practices in various religions, these aromatic symphonies delicately intertwine with the spiritual realm, forging a sublime connection with the divine. The ethereal essence of one's being, commonly known as the soul, is profoundly stirred by the captivating power of fragrance to awaken sentiments, reminisce cherished memories, and transport one to the world beyond the ordinary.

The essence of fragrance possesses the enchanting power to stir the depths of one's being, serving as a gentle whisper that evokes the splendor and intricacy of existence. Like a delicate blossom unfurling its petals, the ethereal essence of a blooming flower dances upon the air, captivating our senses and transporting us to a realm of pure olfactory bliss. The warm embrace of freshly baked bread, its intoxicating aroma wafting through the air, evokes a sense of comfort and nostalgia, awakening memories of cherished moments shared around the table. And in the gentle caress of a loved one's perfume, we find solace and connection, as the harmonious blend of notes intertwines with our very being, leaving an indelible mark upon our souls.

The magical essence of fragrance is intimately intertwined with the depths of the subconscious mind, a boundless reservoir brimming with a symphony of thoughts, memories, and emotions. In the realm of olfactory exploration, esteemed neuroscientists have unveiled a captivating revelation: the ethereal essence of scent possesses an extraordinary ability to awaken dormant memories and evoke profound emotions, delicately concealed within the recesses of our subconscious mind.

The ethereal essence of fragrance possesses the captivating ability to subtly sway our emotions and actions, permeating our subconscious realm. In the realm of fragrances, one cannot overlook the captivating allure of lavender and chamomile. These exquisite scents possess a remarkable ability to gently embrace the senses, unveiling a world of tranquilly and serenity. Their harmonious essence has been known to gracefully alleviate stress and anxiety, bestowing upon the beholder a profound sense of calmness. In a delightful contrast, the exhilarating aromas of citrus or peppermint have the remarkable ability to elevate one's vitality and sharpen their concentration. The ethereal dance of our subconscious, entwined with the essence of fragrance, unveils the profound symphony that scent orchestrates upon our delicate psychological tapestry.

Furthermore, the ethereal realm of scent intertwines harmoniously with the art of taste, delicately shaping and enhancing our gastronomic journeys. The olfactory symphony of culinary fragrances orchestrates a harmonious dance upon our senses, transforming the act of dining into a multisensory masterpiece. The alluring aroma of a meticulously crafted culinary creation possesses the power to awaken our gustatory desires, while an unappealing fragrance can evoke a contrary response.

Transcending its mere influence on the individual, fragrance possesses the exquisite ability to intertwine our very essence with the vast embroidery of the universe. In the realm of olfactory artistry, one must acknowledge the ethereal nature of fragrance molecules, delicate particles gracefully released into the atmosphere, where they dance and intertwine, ultimately merging with the very essence of the air itself. In such a manner, the fragrances we come across intertwine with the symphony of our surroundings, forging a harmonious bond between ourselves, the natural realm, and the celestial expanse.

Moreover, the exquisite incorporation of fragrances in sacred rituals and timeless traditions across myriad cultures serves as a testament to the profound reverence for a transcendent essence that gracefully envelops every sentient being. This concept evokes the notion that fragrance serves as a vessel, not merely for the ethereal, but also for the harmonious interplay between all living beings and the very fabric of the cosmos.

The essence of fragrance goes past mere pleasant aromas, for it serves as a delicate bridge that unites our soul, the depths of our subconscious mind, the vessel of our physical being, and the boundless expanse of the universe. Its ethereal essence delicately weaves through the quilt of our spiritual rituals, evoking a profound sense of transcendence. Like a fragrant whisper, it stirs the depths of our subconscious, awakening dormant memories that dance in harmony with our being. Its aromatic embrace caresses our physical form, bestowing upon us a renewed sense of vitality and balance. And in its enchanting presence, we find ourselves intricately intertwined with the very fiber of existence, a symphony of scents that binds us to the world in a mesmerizing embrace. By immersing ourselves in the enchanting world of fragrance, we unlock the profound wisdom that resides within, unravelling the intricate strings that weave our being into the grand blanket of existence. In the realm of olfactory artistry, fragrance takes on a transformative essence, embarking upon a sensory odyssey that surpasses the boundaries of our corporeal perceptions. It bestows upon us a profound communion with the ethereal realms of the soul, intellect, physique, and the very fabric of the cosmos.

After 15 years in the industry, I have come to appreciate perfumery as a vast ocean of precious gems. There is always more to discover and new techniques to master. This passion never fails to captivate and enthrall me. As an apprentice perfumer, I can attest to the fact that our industry is not just a means of earning a living, but rather a way of life that requires dedication and a unique mindset to fully embrace and appreciate.

Only you, your essence, your psyche, and no one else can manifest this ardor. As a professional, I have come to understand that attuning oneself to the innate beauty of nature is the most exquisite art form, and indeed, the essence of life itself.

A fragrance embarks on a journey, passing through countless hands, minds, and souls, fighting to assert its very essence. As perfumers, we are merely vessels through which fragrances can journey and find their true expression.

9 789360 702540

Printed at Repro India Ltd.